FAMILY MATTERS

The Principles & Roles of Family

By

Terry Kellogg, M.A.

BRAT Publishing, 369 Montezuma Street - Suite 203, Santa Fe,
New Mexico 87501
1-800-359-BRAT (2728) or 505-662-9200   FAX 505-662-4044

Kellogg, Terry
FAMILY MATTERS

ISBN 1-880257-11-4

Printed in the United States of America

BRAT Publishing, 369 Montezuma Street - Suite 203,
Santa Fe, NM 87501
1-800-359-BRAT (2728) or 505-662-9200   FAX 505-662-4044

♦♦♦ Books offered by BRAT Publishing:

Broken Toys Broken Dreams *Understanding and Healing Codependency, Compulsive Behaviors and Family* Terry Kellogg

attrACTIVE WOMEN *A Physical Fitness Approach To Emotional & Spiritual Well-Being* Marvel Harrison & Catharine Stewart-Roache

Finding Balance *12 Priorities For Interdependence And Joyful Living* Kellogg Harrison Family & Relationship Series

Family Gatherings - More Family Matters - *The Issues & Traits of Family* Terry Kellogg

Pathways to Intimacy *Communicating With Care & Resolving Differences* Kellogg Harrison Family & Relationship Series

The Sacred Trust *The Parenting & Guardianship of Children and Creating Healthy Families* Kellogg Harrison Family & Relationship Series

♦♦♦ Inspirational & Gift Books offered by BRAT Publishing:

Butterfly Kisses *Little Intimacies For Sharing!* Harrison & Kellogg & Michaels

Hummingbird Words *Self Affirmations & Notes To Nurture By* Harrison & Kellogg & Michaels

Roots & Wings *Words On Growing A Family* Harrison & Kellogg & Michaels

Reflections *Guideposts and Images For The Journey* Harrison & Kellogg & Michaels

On Eagle's Wings *Words And Images for Your Spirit To Soar* Kellogg & Harrison & Firth

♦♦♦ Also Available from BRAT Publishing:

marvel notes™ *Elegant & delightful greeting cards*

Educational videos and audios on families and relationships

DEDICATION

To Marvel
Soulmate, Playmate, & Helpmate

PREFACE

The idea of the influences of early family and childhood experience on later life, though not new, has only been explored with much detail since the 1950's. Literature, however, has always been filled with stories of joy and tragedy centered around intergenerational family issues and personal childhood experiences impacting the characters. Past psychoanalysts, including Freud, have referenced the link between childhood trauma and adult symptomology, but a systematic approach to the theme of family has evolved primarily in the past four decades. The real pioneers of family systems theory are the handful of therapists and theorists who were writing and teaching in the late fifties, and some are still at it. Virginia Satir was perhaps best known and frequently quoted, but Jackson, Haley, Bowen, Montalvo, Whitaker, Minuchen and Erikson covered a similar time span.

A second generation cropped up in the 1970's and 1980's. This generation of therapists expanded on the earlier work, some integrated emotional process and addiction theory into the systems approach. It was in this period that I began my work in training, counseling and teaching. The return of the Viet Nam vets, and work with them in the late seventies and early eighties, while also setting up programs for families with chemical dependency and abuse, presented me with the stark reality of the severe impact of past trauma on present life. New research and thinking is further helping us define and understand family trauma and its echoes.

Much of what follows is a blend of theory and research in a form attempting to avoid oversimplification which supports denial and stereotyping, while also avoiding a pedantic, diagnostic research style that few can follow. For over twenty-five years I have worked with a diverse group of families with various problems and backgrounds. My experience in addiction recovery, domestic abuse projects, sexual trauma, adolescent counseling, couples work, grief counseling, and family systems theory, as well as graduate work in History, English, Education, and Human Development have entered this book, but the real source has been the thousands of individuals who have shared their experiences in therapy or as Kellogg's Lifeworks™ participants. Though only a few actual stories are included, the essence of their sharing is reflected. The following pages are infused with their hope and courage. Hopefully this book will provide a foundation for an understanding of the concept and dynamics of family systems.

CONTENTS

FAMILY MATTERS
The Principles & Roles of Family

SECTION I
PRINCIPLES OF FAMILY SYSTEMS

INTRODUCTION

Our roots are planted in our family-of-origin or creation. When
we are firmly grounded we can spread our wings and soar.

Roots & Wings

The advent of the computer age forced a culture to think in
terms of systems. Everything must be systematized before pro-
gramming is effective. Social systems theory grew up as com-
puters proliferated. The term 'system' reflects the relationships,
reactions, additions and workings of components in a reverberating
manner. Now there are ecosystems, economic systems, bio-systems,
transportation and telecommunication systems, sound systems, mechanical systems, agri-systems and so on. A family is a system. This
system can be like a web, and we, like a fly, caught in the middle of
the spider's web.

A primary traditional function of family has been to create an
environment of safety and learning, a place for children to grow
through the dependency stages and move from family to be productive members of society and create a family with their children.
Family exists to ensure continuation of the species, transmission of
basic knowledge, the protection of the vulnerable and the productivity of the group or clan. It is a place of provision, not just of physical
need but of nurturing, meaning, and safety. Most of what is true
about families is true of social systems. Community, neighborhood,
school, corporation, state or nation all operate on principles of social
system's theory.

CHAPTER 1
On The Family

The gentle cherishing of all forms of life come with accepting life
as a single community sharing the same home and hearth.

Reflections

Family is a collection of patterns, not an independent reality. It is a blend of biology, society, belief and myth. The term family describes various combinations of persons who are in relationship with one another as family members. A nuclear or biological family group consists of father, mother and biological offspring. This has variations such as one parent with offspring from different partners. Often a couple without offspring is called a family or 'married couple.' In the United States the term *family* is applied to a group of two or more persons related by blood, marriage, or adoption, and residing together. Traditionally there has been a designated head of household, usually the oldest adult man. This designation has been less focused on in the past few decades.

An extended family group includes various relationships and relatives of different generations. They are a residential family group when living under the same roof. A kindred group involves a bond of family or family spirit. In many cultures the blood bond or lineage is dominant over the sexual bond or marriage. The adjustment of children raised in the United States depends greatly on the relational adjustments of parents, but in other cultures as well as many families in the United States, the major influences are spread over many relatives and generations, positive and negative.

In human relationships there is always divergence and rebellion matched with structure and conformity around the institutionalizing of the connections. The impact of these variations along with the basic drives, urges, and impulses of humans make the precise defining and predicting of family systems process impossible.

Family structure is influenced by historical process and descriptions of family at various periods of the past. Within our present culture are seeds of the traditional ancient Hebrew family, Greco-Roman family influences, feudal and Renaissance families, the industrial age family, agrarian and frontier, myth and reality, as well as depression, post war, and post feminist movement processes. Even now the developmental changes as men's awareness is impacting family.

A movement and awareness taking hold is called Pro Natalism. This is a position of noticing, protecting and advocating for healthy children and strong support for the needs of children. The pro natalist movement is approaching the political/cultural issues such as how we view children, child protection, health care, day care and community involvement. It is also deeply concerned with impacting family dynamics along similar lines including child rearing, safer and stress reduced family environment, and moral development. This is the basic approach held by the author and editor of this book.

Family is impacted by society just as it impacts society. Authoritarian families could predispose members to form totalitarianism politics but an authoritarian state may also produce patriarchal or dominant parent family life. Democratic political process will influence the cultural family dynamics toward more group sharing and less patriarchy. These influences are gradual and not universal as they may conflict with other traditions including religious practice. Economic setting and change also determines the family structure. Family structure is altered by depression as well as times of plenty. Currently, to maintain a level of life style many families must alter their structure. These changes include fewer children and two working adults because of economics. Economic prosperity is likely to be accompanied by birth rate increases. Religion has a profound impact on family structure, size, and practice.

Family changes are wrought by prevailing thoughts, beliefs, and feelings on human development, personality formation, value orientation, and beliefs in the purpose or function of family. These are further impacted by several influences including technology, (fertility control as an example), leisure time, children as economic assets or liabilities, and so on.

The common threads in family include the reproductive and companionship functions. Family also functions in areas of recreation, status, education, protection, religious practice, economic security, jealousy control, and fulfillment of basic dependency, worth, and belonging needs. Clifford Kirkpatrick outlines four fundamental factors impacting human institutions as well as individuals: natural environment, heredity, culture, and variable responses.

Natural environment such as climate, resources, soil, plant and animal life impact and limit style of living and family dynamics. *Heredity* includes the genetic peculiarities engendering adaptive traits and reinforce bonds but also the genetic aberrations effecting the ability to be accepted or bond. *Culture* includes the social norms, impressions and values. Material cultures are tools, transportation devices, and building. Social culture is knowledge, belief and custom. *Variable responses* include the non-institutionalized or unexpected interactions, those not part of the culture. A child may be rejected because of a similarity to a hated relative. A member of a family may contract a disease or become mentally ill. Each of these characteristics is interacting with the others in complex and ongoing ways to form the family system.

Problems may stem from scarcity, inferiority or rejection because of differences, competition or clashes, including conflicting values or goals, cultural inconsistency, such as belief in equality and discrimination practices, or mixed cultural conflicts often seen in periods of large immigration.

Individual maladjustments often stem from childhood experiences and problems in family life. Problems can also stem from forces beyond family influences in environment, genetics, culture or non-familial variable responses. Even when the impact is external the family is still the resource for our coping or maladjustment to these problems. A study of family will hopefully facilitate a more adaptive posture, even though family is not always the source of conflict.

The current concept of family is an extension of the need to evolve toward meaning and value. Each person holds mental and emotional images of family, often conflicting. Each person creates and participates in family in their own unique way. The definition and image is not only of individual family but of the understanding of family as a broad cultural concept. These images may set up unrealistic expectations, limit one's participation and subvert the possibilities.

Images of family vary. One member may have a very different felt sense, meaning, definition of family than another member. The needs, feelings, connections, and inclusions of family vary as well.

These stem from differences of all types - age, development, personality, character, role, and so on. Regional, cultural and ethnic differences are considerable regarding family. The image of family also changes with the view. What is seen varies depending on the angle, light, time of viewing, unique experiences of the viewer, and the cognitive and emotional lenses viewed through.

Family supports biological, social, and conceptual patterns. Families are governed by social principles, operate within premises and involve variations in membership. Family is not contained within its patterns, principles, premises and members but these create a value called family. Family is a community defined less by geography than by commitment and bond. Ancestry and marriage are two important defining aspects but many families are more inclusive while others are more exclusive.

Family is often described as the building block of community and community is the construction framework for families. If community seems to be deteriorating one must obviously look closely at the construction material, the building blocks. International and political approaches to family and family values are generally unfocused and unclear. Each advocate and proponent for change or tradition is basing their energies on their own unique vision, definition, and experience. Pro family movements have not necessarily advocated healthy family life. The concept of family values, recently a political slogan, is nebulous and not necessarily a movement toward value. The idealized family often referred to is not necessarily healthy nor does it fit the needs and awareness of the culture, but often fits the political needs and aspirations of a group or individual.

Family is a battered and fractured concept. Over one half of the people in the United States no longer live in the traditional family setting with two parents and children in one house. The reality and health of traditional models must be examined and advocacy must allow flexibility for the great diversity of need and meaning.

Past personal family influences can exert a firm grip on present reality. Understanding the concepts, issues, and principles of family will help individuals resolve the reverberations of past family experience and allow the freedom to create a family in accord with personal hopes and values. Family is the first setting of bonding and community. When family has been a place of nurturing and safety, members are better able to evolve individually on a path of choice and consequence, they are more likely to participate positively in community. When family has been a place of pain, confusion or conflict, one must embark on a process of resolution before moving toward healthy connections.

Almost everyone has been a part of a family, and many have spent their entire existence in the fold of a single family. How has family experience impacted individual choices and life styles and what hold does past family experience still have over the present?

The functions of family are many. A couple becomes a family and offers companionship and meaning to their lives. Children may arrive and the family becomes the vehicle by which they learn to survive, prosper and function in society. Family is a place to develop the esteem and learn the skills to ensure personal survival as well as the survival of our species and planet. Now, more than ever, is the nurturing and noticing of family essential. Without it humans may pollute, consume, and battle their way out of existence. This generation can learn about family and utilize the learning to build healthier families. Family is the primary teaching institution and the spiritual soul of culture. It is also a culture of its own. When the family culture is weak, the members are vulnerable to gangs, destructive relationships and cults. Members act out the absence of healthy bonding and modeling through addiction, isolation or other destructive ways. When the family is broken the culture is broken.

It is important to understand and resolve the issues of family of origin. The losses must be completed and grieved, the violence debriefed and the covert and denied pathology dealt with to be able to dwell fully in the present and maintain balance and intimacy. The courage and strength of family members committed to health can be built upon and passed on to future generations. Most recursive adult pathology is a reaction to, or a reenactment of, unresolved issues from the past.

Destructiveness toward self or others in the absence of threat is not natural to our species. It is an acting out of hurt, loss, trauma, or imbalance that sustains itself by creating more of the same. Most cultural violence and destructiveness is a direct consequence of a brokenness of family. The broken family causes a broken culture spawning more broken family. The spiral continues until it is reversed by individual awareness.

The prevalent and *perceived* media modeling of family has been idealized television. The *real* modeling came from childhood. *In childhood we learn whether family is a harbour of safety or a setting of stress.* The realities and stories of family shape concepts and tolerance levels - stories of biblical families, with fratricide, incest and severe low functioning; stories of pioneer families, often stark, hard working and tragic; family saga mini-series, with high drama and passion; TV sitcoms, with innocuous 'made for TV' and easily resolved problems, and more recently high cynicism and low morality; news media and talk show families with a focus on bizarre and extreme circumstances all have an impact on how we view family. Culturally we have been taught a patriarchal, religious, overly consumptive, upwardly mobile, fast track system filled with contradictions and impossibilities. We are now seeing more brash, competitive, trash talking, cynical, self denigrating symbols of media family. All of it impacts.

The neglect and absence of parenting skills ranks second only to the absence of relationship and intimacy skills in preventing healthy family life. Adults are all too often unprepared due to their own past. Many are untrained, undecided and unwilling to venture through life in a committed, caring, positive posture with a spouse and children. One must go backward to move forward. In understanding the system and resolving the sabotaging messages, destructive modeling, the losses and traumas of the past, the movement toward intimacy and enjoyment of family becomes possible.

We have been told to follow our dream and find our joy, create our own reality. Dream the impossible and we will do the impossible. We can affirm our way to self love and success. Visualize health and it will be ours. Fantasies can be our realities. The voice within is the key to never doing without. Positive thinking, mind control, affirmation, fantasy and creative visualization will help anyone sell real estate or life insurance, but too many of us have sabotaging messages, struggles and stranglings from past events. Unresolved grief and trauma do not allow us to think and grow rich. These tools are effective only after resolving the past!

The following information on family systems may facilitate awareness and open the doors to change and success. Some of the principles overlap. Some require more time to understand and discuss. Each has an impact on identity and choices. Looking at the past generally is a colossal waste of time unless it is linked to present reality and recurrent life issues.

Unfortunately what is said and done throughout these Volumes will have little effect on the lives of people in our culture who are struggling with survival issues and live in poverty, high crime areas or are homeless. Family systems, self esteem, boundaries and spiritual discovery tend to lose significance when each day is spent with most energy directed towards survival. On the other end of the spectrum is the probability that members of our culture who have so much wealth and power and are so far removed from the reality of the lives of most people, will ignore this whole issue or judge it meaningless. The importance of these issues transcends class, economic and ethnic realities, but these realities impact interest and postures toward family matters.

During this present period of technological advance and scientific information overload, thousands of tracts and books are published every day while during that day fifty species of life are wiped out in large part by shortsighted arrogance and ignorance. The burden we leave our children goes beyond financial debt from fiscal irresponsibility and ego, it goes beyond the burdens of family and political conflict. Within this overwhelm of information, technology and conflict our children must learn a new spirituality, discover a broader vision to rise above where we have been toward a deeper connection, to utilize creativity for the enhancement of creation process, to use family as the source of enlightened cherishing of what is vulnerable and what is valuable.

The investment in ignorance in our culture often seems enormous, only in ignorance could people overspend, the base of our consumptive economics, elect the dishonest, and be seduced by pleading politicians and evangelists. Only through ignorance could there be the collusion to violence and destruction of our atmosphere, water, cities, and life. Combating ignorance must be a community struggle when so many forces seem so invested in it. Ignorance is the ultimate censorship. We need not burn books if people cannot read or understand them. Hopefully *Family Matters* will be read and shed a little light and wisdom on family, allowing the door to open for other passages.

Four children grew up in a very small house in a family with a great deal of stress. Alcoholism and violence were regular visitors, silence was a deafening presence, the four children were lost, hurt, and confused.

Without a plan or even awareness the community mobilized. The third child was given special responsibilities at school and was befriended by several nurturing teachers. A local coach picked up the frightened eight year old and taught him baseball, basketball, teamwork, hard work and the joys of belonging for the next six years. A neighbor family virtually adopted him, sharing meals, prayer, family rituals and casual and comfortable acceptance. A local butcher pulled him on skis behind his runabout until the sun disappeared, the butcher's wife prepared picnics, his brother taught him to work out and be strong, his sister taught him to avoid the conflicts and be gentle, an old man who ran the soda fountain gave him a smile, advice, and cherry cokes even when he didn't have the nickel. A classmate in seventh grade taught him to kiss while her father drove them to the movies and then the father put his arm on his shoulder as he walked him back to the house in a fatherly way and winked when he said goodnight. The priest smiled and joked with him when he delivered milk, his eighth grade teacher told him he would do important things with his life.

A community without any meetings, fund raising, or volunteer organizations raised this child and he still belongs to each of them. I am that child and I only hope I can give back some of what I have received.

We are each needed by the children.

The following principles of family systems are the basis for an understanding of family and self.

CHAPTER 2

FIRST PRINCIPLE
The Whole Is Greater Than The Sum Of Its Parts

A healthy family is the foundation for individual development and
healthy community is the basis for family development.

The Sacred Trust

A family is more than its members. Just as a nation or community is more than a collection of people, a family has impact, symbol, and energy beyond its membership. To know us we must know our families and see beyond the individual members. Family includes the rituals, meaning, cultural context, expectations, symbolic representations as well as the hopes, rules, principles and dynamics. When a child leaves a home to go off to school, be married or just on their own, they may miss particular pieces; feeling pain about their room, the family pet, the yard played in. They may also feel a loss of specific daily family relationships, but they still hang on to a sense of family membership. It is still their family and they are an active part of it though now involved with new things. The difference in leaving home with family connection intact and leaving home with a broken family connection is great.

Ken and Charles were assigned to room together their
first year in college. Ken was quite homesick, and in fact
was physically ill for much of the first semester and went
home most weekends even though he lived in the neighboring
state several hundred miles away and going home was not

economical. Members of Ken's family came to visit the weekends he wasn't home. Ken's family, before he went to college had a big farewell party as a send-off with his high school friends and extended family present.

Charles was older. Never talked about home, spent his weekends studying and went for long walks in the nearby woods. His steadiness made Ken feel quite immature. Charles was attending on a GI bill and worked part time in the refectory. Charles had run away from home at six-teen, spent eighteen months on the streets and then joined the service. He had had no contact with any family member since he was sixteen years old.

By the end of the second year, though no longer room-mates, the scenario had altered considerably. Ken was do-ing well in classes, had a steady girlfriend, and was involved in a variety of activities. Charles was still studying and hik-ing but was on medication for depression and never really integrated into student life. His isolation was a continuation of his separateness as a child and the depression was related to the loneliness and deep burden of unresolved childhood scenes of family violence he had run away from at sixteen but had never found or been provided closure on.

Being kicked out, running away or a family going through such radical change or loss that it no longer feels like family puts one on very shaky ground. There is an internal and external disconnection, a breakdown in security, and meaning. To be ostracized, even from a low functioning family is a process many cannot handle and others handle with great difficulty. It is a glib statement often made by counselors and advisers to divorce your family, leave and do not go back - much easier said than done, sometimes unrealistic, often unnecessary and always difficult. It is a suggestion seldom followed for long. Rather than separate from our families we might use time with them to study, learn, understand and grow. We do need separateness from actively abusive family members. Time spent with family may be monitored and charged with a spirit of growth when we notice and record, when we look beyond and make links to our life away from family. We then learn choices.

Jill joined a woman's group with a very strong and well respected local therapist. She had spent the first few weeks telling of her parent's angry relationship and how critical and demanding her mother was of her. She announced she was going home for the holidays and would miss group for the next two weeks. The therapist and group immediately 'jumped on' her case for spending time with her 'crazy' family. They insisted she make a pact with the group to not go home for Christmas, not to call, and just to send a short note to say she was working on personal boundaries and could not be there. Jill complied with everything including getting an answering machine to screen family calls. The family actually took the news quite well and simply let her know if she could find some time after the holidays they hoped to see her. Jill however was miserable, felt alone, and discovered over the holidays most of the group members were with their families and had little time for her neediness. Her therapist was on a cruise with her own parents.

*Jill called the crisis line Christmas eve and was re-
ferred to a therapist who told her to follow her heart and
be wherever she wanted to be for the holidays. She encouraged Jill to spend more time with her favorite sister if she did
go home and to journal her reactiveness to her parent's messages to her and each other. On Christmas day Jill showed
up at home and burst into tears as her sister gave her a
welcoming embrace. She was quite adept at sidestepping
her mother's questions and criticisms for the next four days
and did a great deal of journaling about her parent's marriage.
In her journaling she began to recognize what had happened
in her own marriage was a direct reaction to her fear of
becoming like her mother. She never complained about,
asked for, or needed anything. She was subservient in every respect. She became a nonperson in response to her
mother's overwhelming persona and demandingness. On
her return she was able to process with her new therapist
what she had learned and returned to her group with a much
stronger identity and resolve to follow her heart.*

Marital separation and divorce are difficult family processes
to endure. They involve a loss of dreams, hopes, relationships
and connections. The divorce involves leaving a relationship but
many divorced persons also leave the family. Often a family no longer
seems like family to those left. The depth of pain and trauma in
leaving and being left is something people in the process of divorce
seldom bargain for. It is not in their plans or expectations. A marriage is more than a contract between two persons, just as a family is
more than the marriage or any particular relationship. Both are liv-

ing entities with their own living spirit. The family has form, movement and substance. When split by parting members, the family still remains as something more than the members. The loss can be a fracturing of spirit and a lessening of one's life sense. To lose a family member is a trauma. To lose the belonging to family is a spiritual earth quake with life long tremors.

Maintaining relationship with parts of the system is helpful in lessening the shock. The loss of the wholeness of family, though a common occurrence in our culture, is a severing of the context of our lives. We can grow a new family of creation but like a missing limb, the pain is felt even when the limb is lost.

Jack had spent the last three years at the top of his career. Requests for his expertise were numerous as were the demands on his time. As his travels increased he became more disconnected from friends and community as well as from family. His wife was somewhat jealous of his success and resented his absence. His children were angry as well. His son once said, "When you are gone, I miss you and then I get angry. When you come home if I stay angry, I miss you even more. So I have to give up my feelings to be with you at all."

On one of those trips Jack met someone who was fascinated by his honesty and humility in a field of large egos and personal misrepresentation. She was supportive, friendly, and also well respected in the same field Jack worked in. Jack and his new friend corroborated on a few projects and soon realized the fascination they felt was love, or grew into love, and now choices and decisions needed to be made.

21

Jack had been married nineteen years and to leave his wife seemed inconceivable. He met her right out of high school and married her right out of college, the children came shortly after. After months of agonizing decisions and the beginnings of deception, he made the decision he couldn't live with dishonesty. He decided to leave his marriage.

In ensuing months Jack's decision to leave his wife of nineteen years set off an avalanche of loss from which Jack may never fully recover. He lost his children for most of the next three years, he lost almost all of his friends, he lost his community. His work partners sided with his wife and left with his business. He lost his house, nearly all his possessions including personal goods such as passport, photos, and mementos. He lost his savings and was ordered to pay lifelong support to his former wife who kept him in court and in the legal process entwined with attorneys for most of five years. There were personal gains for Jack, a potential life long relationship filled with meaning and integrity, but the decision to leave his wife precipitated a catastrophe of proportions he couldn't have imagined.

In an era of revolution regarding family and its meaning, in a time of much family bashing and parent blaming, it is easy to miss the importance of belonging. "They may be sick and crazy people but they are *my* sick and crazy people. They may be addicts, mentally disturbed, and grouchy but when push comes to shove, they would sacrifice deeply to keep me safe. They may hurt me, but they would try their best not to let others hurt me, do what they can to help me heal, except perhaps to admit that they hurt me."

Sue was suffering from depression and bulimia. Her family supported her therapy both emotionally and financially. They said they were willing to be as involved as necessary. Sue and her therapist invited the family in for a session. Sue proceeded to blast her family for their phoniness, unavailability, and enabling her mother's chemical dependency. Needless to say, Sue lost their emotional and financial support. Her therapist stuck with her but a lesson was learned. Sue could have processed her feelings and sorted out many of the issues before dealing with her family directly. If the family had not been blasted with this barrage of emotion and overwhelm of information they may have been able to hear more and continued to support her.

A family is the community we learn from and look to for support. It is a community we will defend and usually feel protective of even when we are exposing the pathology. The concept of family is a celebration of growing and changing. The changing does not alter the wonder and wholeness of the family.

The family is more than the collection of its members and their relationships, the parts. When family members gather, the energy is more and different than the total of each member separately. The different parts may be healthy or sick, wild or mild but each family's dynamics are unique. In family therapy a therapist will see considerably more of the system when all members are present, than seeing members over time individually. The group dynamic is like an organism where the separated parts make little sense but together form something with energy, form and function. It can be directed towards constructive or destructive energy. In family systems therapy, therapists may not be able to see the entire family together but try to accumulate enough information about the system to be able to understand it as a whole even while working with its parts. To see the individual, the system must be viewed, the influences that continue to impact.

Fred came in for therapy first, his other three brothers and one sister came later. Every month or so a new one appeared on the appointment calendar. All four were chemically dependent, two on alcohol, two on speed, three were in recovery, one wasn't. There was a fifth child who suicided at age twenty-three.

They had many common problems besides the chemicals. All were underachieving and felt like failures. All experienced temporary relationships and severe bouts of hopelessness. They were also all very protective of both parents who were referred to as 'Saint Mom and Dad.'

It wasn't until the third session with all siblings present the reality of the system and parent's path to sanctity came out. Both parents were good, kind, loving, and never fought or yelled. They lacked any relationship spark and they did not acknowledge anger, so few issues were clarified. But the primary problem came with the recognition of their own sanctity and how they used that to guide and to guilt.

The essential message from the parents to the children was, "We are good, kind, decent, and do not fight. We give our life for you and each other, so you would never do anything that would hurt us. And what would hurt us is if you did anything we didn't want you to do. It would hurt us if you did not become exactly like us or like what we would like you to be."

This was not love. It was guilt, disguised as love. Five children became lost in the heavy ongoing presence of this message of guilt and control.

Leaving family does not leave behind the family system. The system is carried on. Lifestyle and methods of operating are responses to the family of origin. The effect of the whole of families sculpts the whole of our lives. The construction of a family is a process just as is the destruction. Even in the breakdown of family, something of the family remains in each piece and the elements of new construction are built on these. New families and relationships are cloned from the remaining cells of the old.

Nancy remembered saying to a friend she would never be like her mother. Nancy's father was the only physician in a small town and was seldom home. Her mom took his calls, did the books, lived in his shadow, and had little life of her own. Her mom felt sad but always said the needs of the sick came first.

Nancy married a minister, lived in a large city, seldom saw her husband, and lived in his shadow as a minister's wife. She justifying her sadness by saying the needs of the church came first until she became too depressed to keep up the image and finally realized she had followed in her mother's footsteps.

The family system impacts all other systems entered. Individuals are each reflections of the family dynamic, but when the reflections are seen integrally, they reflect a wholeness that is more than the collection of reflections. Families have impact, symbol, energy and history beyond their membership. Even the survival of the family is greater than the survival of individuals. To know ourselves we must know our families and see beyond the individuals. Change and growth in a member may threaten the system, the member may then be sacrificed, evicted from the family. The loss is strange, for even outside they are a part of. The growing and movement expands the parameters and scope of the family. The individual journey is a family movement, one discovers new frontiers pushing the parameters from within or pulling at them from the outside.

Jim's family lived in a depressed mining town in northern Minnesota. The family was close knit and a very powerful covert rule was "everyone lives nearby because Mom would die of loneliness if you left." Jim broke the rule and moved to Australia. He married there and started a mining operation in the southwest. Over the next twenty years most of the family left Minnesota and its sporadic employment opportunities to be a part of Jim's very successful mining operation and to support his efforts to effect a political change in his new land. His mother visited a few times, she never died of loneliness, but she did become filled with pride at the success of her children.

Our spine is only one root of a family tree. From *The Bean Field*, by Barbara Kingsolver, "a scarecrow is only as good as the stick that holds him in the ground." This reflects the impact of the roots of family. When roots run strong and deep the individual can hold up to withstand great pressures and pulls. Deep roots allow the freedom to soar.

Sam had been passed from foster home to foster home after being abandoned by his mom at two and given up finally by his alcoholic father at age three. At eight years old he was diagnosed with Attention Deficit Disorder. He had not completed a successful year at school and was labeled incorrigible. He was adopted into a loving family with several children, great joy and a sense of security. Although he still had some problems socializing, he learned to play the guitar, became a prominent classical guitarist in his early twenties. His musical success enabled him to feel his self worth and was the vehicle by which he was able to connect with others who shared his interest in music. In therapy he eventually began to grieve a loss of his original family and to feel the abandonment issues. He then began to move beyond his social inhibitions and fears of abandonment which prevented his risking in relationships.

Families are resilient, the primary places of rest and refuge in traumatic times. Families are jealous and often controlling, frightening and humiliating, outrageous and frequently hilarious. Humor is the cement of the system. Humorless families fracture easily and do not patch well. Spiritual values form the foundation of the family entity. With weak spiritual foundations and beliefs members fall through and are easily lost. Strong religious practice is not a valid substitute for a weak spirit and wobbly foundation.

Jody's family was very religious, hosting prayer meetings, running the church Sunday school and evening biblical discussions. Jody however was very repressed and unhappy. She shied away from relationships and felt a lot of shame about her body. Her spirit was dampened. She left home for college and disengaged completely from religious practice and prayer. She remained withdrawn and did not take care of herself. She received a Master's degree in social work and began working for a county agency.

In her first week a coworker invited her to a twelve step meeting. She reacted by saying she was not an addict nor was anyone in her family. Her friend said, "Come along anyway. It's for people from low functioning families." Jody protested and defended her family but attended the meeting and continued attending. Her discovery was her family used religion to cover all the problems and feelings much like one might use a drug. Religion was also used to guilt and control.

Her friend became a spiritual guide and mentor who taught her the difference between religion and spirituality. Jody returned to church but found one that celebrated and accepted. She is still healing the damage done to her spirit and still learning to enjoy her body while discovering the strength in integrating her feelings and intellect.

Families are neither left easily nor created easily. As new families are created they too will be more than the sum of their parts and their builders.

Families create the paradigm of reality and enclosure from which the individual operates. Cutting off from an aspect of the system or a member is common, but to stand outside of the paradigm and see through a different lens is a seldom accomplished feat. Family is viewed through and within the system itself. It is judged by its own premises while its rules continue and roles reappear. Other organizations are viewed from the paradigm of families. Families offer a way of reacting to and understanding other systems.

Bill was smaller than his siblings and had red hair. He was teased a great deal and felt like the odd duck, never fitting in. This feeling carried into school and when he left to enter the corporate world he succeeded but still never felt accepted nor believed he fit in. He started therapy and attended a men's group. In group he finally confessed he just didn't feel like he fit in and wasn't accepted. The feedback he received reflected something far different. He was liked and seemed to fit in, but he kept pulling back from people when they tried to get close. It was when he decided he was out, that he was really out. He prejudged every system he was in by the experience of his own family, and even set up a reenactment of his family experience in other systems and with other people.

It is hard to play a game when we have never known the rules or been on the board. The family is the playing board for career and relationship as well as the method by how the personal universe is organized. Dealing with the wholeness instead of focusing on the parts offers us a chance for detachment and integration. A deeper awareness of format enables navigation through the maze of conscious and unconscious pressure toward a realization of self and a freedom of being. Awareness of the whole system allows choices as to which aspects are hindering and which are facilitating the life path. Choice comes from this awareness.

Mary loved her family but was experiencing problems in her life with her husband and her children. She believed the family she came from was very caring and loving, but she feared her own feelings and could not share them with others. One day she finally realized that her mother had suffered from severe PMS and went emotionally out of control regularly. Mary's response to her mother's erratic emotional behavior was to develop a fear and place a tight wrap around her own feelings keeping everyone including her own children distant. Her loneliness wasn't necessary but a covert reaction to a piece of her family system she had not acknowledged.

New families include the wholeness of the old, blended with life changes and compromised with the system of new partners. In seeing the wholeness, new and healthy systems can grow, allowing members freedom of self discovery in a context of support, strength and integrity. Integrity comes from integral, the single one wholeness of a consistent solid system. When the whole is fractured and operating on conflicting levels, integrity is difficult to achieve. Recognition of the wholeness of family is the primary step in acceptance of more universal deep connections and belonging.

CHAPTER 3

SECOND PRINCIPLE
Components Are The Relationships Between Family Members, Not The Members Themselves

Respect Rituals, Notice Creation, Share Gratitude,
Join in a Spiritual Journey

Butterfly Kisses

A family of five members does not have five components, it has twenty-five components - each person's relationship with themselves and their relationship with the four other family members. Even if a spouse or parent is no longer around, the relationship with the missing person still dwells within the remaining members. Some relationships are more integral to family functioning than others, just as in a mechanical system some components are more important to the functioning. In a car engine with a fouled spark plug the car will run, though miss a little, but if a piston has seized the engine won't run at all nor will it run very long with a clogged fuel line.

A most important relationship in family is the parent relationship, the source of fuel to the family, the power of the engine. The marriage is the foundation and safety net of the family. The marriage represents more than the relationship between the two persons. The marriage represents the history, the meaning, creation, and reason for the family, It represents the process of family building while the individual marriage partners represent the two tracks of family history.

Don and Carla seemed to have a wonderful marriage, but they were faking it. Over time their children began to act out and underachieve. Finally, at the suggestion of a friend Don and Carla entered marriage therapy and addressed the deeper relationship problems they'd denied for a long time because they were both afraid of being alone. Each of them had been raised by single moms who had given up on ever having a healthy relationship.

Their fear was if their problems ever came to surface they would have to split up and live the rest of their life alone. It turned out their problems were able to be resolved, especially after they addressed their fear of being left. The fear was the primary problem. As they began to enjoy their relationship their children began to act out less and to achieve more.

Marriage is built upon the relationship of each marriage partners' relationship with themselves. From healthy identity flows the ability to form and maintain intimate connection. Children learn intimacy more by seeing it modeled than by adults being intimate with children. The Family Issues section of *Family Gatherings* goes further into family relationships, especially the marriage and the sibling relationships.

Children tend to do better in a family where they are less focused on and the adults work at adult relationship. When the adult relationship falls apart or terminates, the focus and needs of the adult often centers on the children. A marriage relationship rests on each marriage partner's personal identity strength, the relationship with self is the real foundation of intimacy with others. Through the relationship with self, intimacy is discovered and healthy parenting is possible. Woody Allen once said, "In our relationships we try to have all of the things we had in childhood and all of the things we didn't have." That makes it difficult.

Rita was torn between her desire for independence and her desire for intimacy. She had married her high school sweetheart but regularly pushed him away to assert her independence. She had been her mom's best friend, but her mom found a new career late in life and pushed her away. Rita admired her mom's career and independence but at the same time was jealous of it. Her conflict came in valuing and wanting again the closeness she felt with her mother and wanting to be like her mother in terms of the modeled independence and toughness, not needing anyone.

Rita finally realized her mother had run away from adult relationships and the fear of being hurt again, first of all by over bonding with her own daughter and later by being obsessed with career and avoiding intimacy through that obsession. Eventually she realized her mother had smothered her, and part of why Rita was pushing her husband away was the fear he would use her and smother her the way her mother had. She finally decided intimacy with her husband didn't threaten her identity nor her independence. This decision allowed her to take risks with her husband's support, risks she had not have been able to take on her own before her awareness.

Relationship maintenance is a primary need of social systems. Low functioning aspects of families often stem from unresolved relationship issues. Different relationships have different functions and the functions may vary and be switched around. Siblings may parent each other or children may participate in major decisions. Relationship is part of why the whole is greater than the sum of its parts. The whole includes additional family components such as the relationships of parents with their parents and siblings. Two people don't get married, six do! Our parents and our partner's parents are part of our relationships with each other. A relationship may involve multiple parents or past marriages. Often the unresolved feelings of these relationships effects family functioning.

Components in a family system are added but not often lost. Some components distract from others but all are important. Sibling relationship problems can distract from the marriage problems and may add tension to the marriage but more often the marriage relationship is acted out by children and the focus is shifted toward the sibling issues. The marriage relationship sets the tone of the relationship with and between siblings.

Tony and Jane were the two oldest children of five. They fought regularly driving the family crazy. Mom and Dad would often argue, but usually about Tony and Jane. In family counseling it was exposed how Tony and Jane were just the distraction. They were acting out mom and dad's fight and mom and dad's fight wasn't so much with each other but with themselves. Their anger and defensiveness came from their own painful childhood experiences they both came to deny. Tony and Jane's job in the family was to distract mom and dad from their pain and to give them something they could be angry about without it threatening the marriage.

The identity of a family is the relationship of the family with itself. Positive relationship is a creation of positive identity for the family and the family members. Family pride, loyalty, consideration and uniqueness are included in relationship issues. Belonging is a primary need. When the belonging is present and nurtured the family and individual strengths are deepened.

Boundaries are a function of family relationship allowing the bonds to deepen or become a source of friction. Family relationships are the source of attachment learning. The earliest sense of belonging is to family. Damaged early attachments and broken belonging are reflected in subsequent relationships. Survival and security are attached to family members. When these attachments are tenuous or broken, survival is threatened and survival solutions are formed. These survival solutions may use an attachment to persons, processes or substances offering a sense or illusion of ensured survival and security while numbing the internal anxiety of threatened survival. Survival solutions may be extremely dependent relationships, avoidance, distraction or any mental or behavioral activity facilitating our movement through threatening times and situations. They include addictive disorders, people pleasing, withdrawal, fantasy, rituals, isolation, dissociation, control, intellectualizing and compulsions.

Everything in Ralph's family had been denied. The root of the problem was always covered with words, excuses and rationalizations. Ralph developed a fixation on words. He wanted to know their roots, he wanted to know the meaning and how words were used. He drove people away. He always felt like he needed to understand something beyond what was said, beyond the words used, to feel sane. He felt a great relief when he finally understood the root meaning of words and what was said. But it was never enough because the real need was to understand what was being denied and covered with words, as the root problem of his family.

Ralph's brother avoided conversation and words, he relied on isolation and withdrawal. His solution to problems was to not face them, to numb out. His sister compulsively overate. She ate her anger, her stress and her fears. All of these behaviors represented survival solutions, reactions to the dilemmas and stress of living in a high denial system where mom was depressed and dad angrily detached. Both parents were college professors who used words and passive aggressiveness to avoid the reality of their problems.

Family over attachment causes its own set of anxieties and repetitions. Dependent relationships, narcissism, and helplessness stem from over bonding within family. Broken relational bonds can cause an internal self-brokenness reflected in internalized shame, distorted beliefs, low self worth and damaged dependency. The broken bond may also set up anxiety and fear based lifestyles and patterns of connecting.

Strong family bonds provide the basis for intimacy and healthy risk taking. The complexity of family relationships is preparation for us to be able to sustain and nurture a variety of relationships in adult life. The trust in healthy family relationship facilitates trusting and intimacy while providing the safety to build healthy self relationship. Relationships are further discussed in *Family Gatherings*, Family Issues Section.

CHAPTER 4

THIRD PRINCIPLE
What Affects One, Affects All

Our difficulties with ourselves befall those closest to us
Reflections

Virginia Satir first described the family as a mobile. A system with the various parts connected and hanging in balance. When a disturbance or force upsets any section of the mobile, the entire mobile begins to react and reverberate to the force. Tension on one part of the mobile is comparable to the stress or problems particular members or relationships in the family may experience. The entire family reacts to the member or the strained relationship. When a family member experiences a trauma, the trauma is shared by the family who witness and often support the person through the difficult time. Each member of a family needs support and process time when one or more members are experiencing stress or crisis. In families with multiple crises or traumas a member may develop a survival mode or altered tolerance for the stress causing them and causing the family to miss or minimize the impact of the crisis on their life. They don't show the reaction, or they react in such a way as to cover it. One may become more successful or more calm as the crisis or terror deepens, but the screen of calm is merely a shield reflecting deeper damage.

Bill's father began drinking again after twenty-six years of alcohol abstinence and sobriety. Bill said it didn't bother him now, although it did when he was growing up. However over the next several months Bill became more and more detached from his wife and children. He was close to getting fired from his job for poor performance before he realized he had many of feelings he was suppressing. The suppression was altering his focus and his ability to connect. His father was still important to him, and his father's recent bout with his alcoholism triggered the childhood terror and anxiety as well as anger.

Reactions to family issues continue long after moving away from the family. The reactions often manifest themselves in low functioning coping mechanisms, addictions, self destructive behaviors, relationship problems, perfectionism and a long list of other possible symptoms. The impact of family problems which began after leaving the family is easier to minimize but often still deep.

For most person's family members are important as are their feelings and hopes. Member's lives continue to impact each other. Often a stressful event in family of origin will trigger older reactions to past events.

John's father was arrested for a hit-and-run accident and cited for driving under the influence. When John heard about this, he began to remember scenes of violence and terror from his childhood although he was now in his late forties. He remembered several incidents of the police arriving at his home in the middle of the night after having been called during episodes of his father battering his mother. John began to experience the insomnia and startle responses he thought he had left behind. As he shared his memories, verbally and emotionally his symptoms were again quieted.

Acknowledging the impact of the lives and process of family members enables one to link the consequences of their stressors to one's own life problems and gives the opportunity to debrief and feel the response. When the responses are repressed they covertly erode quality of life or the health of current relationship.

Acceptance of the impact of the issues of other family members enables a management of responses. Denial of impact involves the risk of shutting down too much emotional awareness and sensitivity and effecting a false withdrawal and real sense of isolation.

Human survival is in part sustained through the feelings of bonding and loyalty to family. Protectiveness, painful reactions to the suffering of others and celebrations of success are natural responses. So is jealousy or wanting to inflict pain when family is or has been a place of hurt. We cannot *not* respond to the people around us and they will invariably respond to our life processes and issues.

Julie used to beat her sister regularly. She hated her sister's attention getting seduction and drive to achieve. The distance between them was finally bridged when Julie began to understand the scapegoat role she played set her up to see her sister as the villain. In fact, Julie's mother had projected horrible pain and anger on Julie, and Julie in turn had projected that pain and anger toward her sister. She also finally accepted her sister's pain as real. Even though her sister overachieved and appeared successful she was still deeply hurt.

She now enjoys seeing her sister's popularity while realizing with empathy that popularity doesn't take away the painful feelings and the deep sense of isolation. Her sister also finally acknowledged she had a need for Julie's admiration and approval, but when she focused on it, always backfired because it escalated the jealousy. Julie and her sister both had used their anger at each other to keep distance so they wouldn't have to feel the family pain.

Illness, divorce, depression, self destructive behavior, addiction, financial problems, suicidal thoughts or attempts, relationship problems, job loss, injury and accident, victims of crime, stressors from our siblings, children, or children's children all impact the extended family. Some members are impacted more than others, but all are affected in some way. Witnessing the trauma, stresses, and losses of family members is experiencing them. *We cannot not be affected by what we witness.*

Jean came from a large high functioning family. Nurturing flowed in abundance from parents to children and grandchildren. The only hitch may have been in grandma's and grandpa's relationship which was loving and respectful but not really intimate and supportive.

After years of planning and hoping Jean became pregnant. The room was decorated, everything was in order and everyone was excited as babies were very highly valued. The baby died during the birth even though it was healthy. The loss was deep and the entire family came to the aid and support of Jean and her husband Bill. In shifts family members took a week or two off their schedules to spend with the grieving couple.

After a few months the would be parents were doing well and looking forward to another pregnancy. The rest of the family had crashed, however. In their witnessing for the couple's deep loss they too experienced it. The family members gave so much but received nothing to help them through their shock, loss of hopes and grieving. In a family session grandma and grandpa who had been especially estranged since the infant's death acknowledged how they felt the loss almost as deeply as the parents. Each sibling shared their feelings and told of the stress, anxiety and impatience they experienced for the past several months. Out of the session came some sharing of the impact of the grandparent's relationship in each of the family members. The children told of their hurt for they knew their parents were lonely. For the first time in forty years grandpa began sobbing and telling of his loneliness, his wife of four decades came over and held him while they shared tears.

A deep relief can occur when family members acknowledge their issues and seek help and support. It is difficult to resolve response feelings and reactions when the issue remains denied. Attempts to hide or deny the impact of the tension in other family members sets up repression of the feelings and responses. The responses and feelings then control. Recognizing responses allows detachment.

Detachment takes place when the problems of others do not set up acting out or loss of balance. Feelings and caring remain, adjustments are made, help offered, but the other family members do not crash with the problem holder. Detaching may require a tough love posture, further involvement or help depends on if the person with the issue is willing to allow the help and do their part. Enabling and over worrying about someone who refuses to change brings one into the problem as part of the problem. Being affected by family members does not require being abused, used or destroyed by them.

Martha's mom gave her free room and board, did not insist on any real help with the household chores or put limits on her access to the labors of other family members. Martha was using drugs, seduction, friends and family. No one outlined consequences or alternatives. When Martha's mom was hospitalized finally for depression and stress, she was given an ultimatum by her physician that included dealing with Martha. She had to offer Martha the choice of drug rehabilitation followed by work, school, or both, or moving out immediately. Martha moved away for three and one half years.

Martha and her mom met for lunch or talked on the phone occasionally, but mom held firm. Mom's health improved but Martha's did not. The family became closer and Martha's two younger brothers took on more responsibility eventually finished college. Martha recently met a former boyfriend who was in recovery and she began attending twelve-step meetings. She may make it, but if she does not, she will not bring down an entire family. Martha's mom now also recognizes her enabling posture toward her children was in part why they became helpless and dependent. They felt useless, overly dependent and had little motivation since under the guise of good mothering they had everything provided and had to do virtually nothing for themselves.

Self care insures we are available to help when help can be accepted. An inability or unwillingness to accept help by the problem bearer does not preclude the need to seek support or help for oneself when family members are experiencing crisis or stress. The impact of the losses, hurts, or acting out befalls each member. The tendency to isolate in response to family tension diminishes the ability for healthy connections.

CHAPTER 5

FOURTH PRINCIPLE
Covert Issues Cause Overt Dynamics

We are driven by what is hidden. The covert causes compulsion.
Broken Toys Broken Dreams

Family secrets are usually not very secret, but rather hazy reflections of denial. All denial within family is eventually acted out or reacted to by members. Moving back to the analogy of the mobile, all the pieces are in balance until tension comes along and strikes at one part of the mobile with considerable force. While holding the part that was impacted and preventing it from moving, the rest of the mobile is still reacting, often vigorously. The rest of the mobile is reverberating to the tension, but the source of the tension isn't reflecting it. The cross pieces of the mobile represent family bonds. In a low functioning family these bonds often become enmeshment. Enmeshment is the loss of boundary sense, an entanglement into the issues and space of others.

Often in family, the person with the tension, the acting out behavior, addiction, mental illness, or struggle, manages to hide or deny. This cover up doesn't lessen the impact on other members, it just makes the other members of the family 'feel crazy' or confused because they don't know why or to what they are reacting. They are enmeshed in a process they cannot consciously sort out.

Lou had been having affairs since his first year of marriage.
His three teenage children were in crisis, his wife depressed.

His oldest daughter had recently messed up a wonderful relationship with her true love, by cheating on him with a casual friend who she really did not care about. Lou's secret was causing stress and acting out throughout the family. When his youngest son was labeled incorrigible the entire family went into counseling. The secret came out and the family began feeling sane. Gradually the acting out behaviors of family members began to lessen. Each family member realized they were reacting to the stress of Lou's addictive behaviors. Both Lou and his wife in doing their family of origins work also began to realize that each of them had a parent who was having secret affairs.

Secret stressors may be denied but they are not really secret, for they are being responded to by each member of the family. Much of therapy involves making the present and past, covert issues explicit so choices can be made. As long as they are covert, these issues cause more of a compulsive need to react. *We are driven by the hidden.* Once it becomes overt and visible, reactions and options may be chosen. Seeing, accepting, and knowing a parent is an alcoholic allows more choices about using alcohol or other substances to medicate feelings, as well as awareness and understanding of the impact of the family disease on the individual. Seeing the dishonesty in family, knowing a family member is depressed and suicidal, allows decisions about responses. When denied, enmeshment is set up and the problem is acted out or reacted to without the ability to resolve or process.

The overt can be dealt with and can be seen, the covert holds in its grip and causes the absence of choice found in compulsive behaviors. It is very 'crazy making' when our parent's relationship is filled with anger or hate, but they pretend caring and loving. The reality presented doesn't match what is felt of the hate and distance. Input and instinct don't jive. Family members always know at some level what is going on in the family even when denied or hidden, not consciously but in other ways.

The secrets of marital problems becomes the reality of anger and distance among the children and subsequent intimacy disorders and damaged identity and trust for family members.

The sexual secrets become sexual fears, shame, repression, dysfunction, compulsion, abuse and infidelity in the following generations.

The secrets of dishonesty set up continued dishonesty and secret keeping, often acted out in shoplifting, lying and cheating by children.

The secrets of hopelessness and suicidality echo in the lives of family members in their feelings of despair, depression, self destructiveness and suicidal attempts or ideation.

There is only one dysfunction, denial, the rest are problems. The denial may be of the problem, of aspects of the problem, the impact of the problem, feelings about it or its long term effects on one's life. Denial precludes the possibility of solving the problems thus causing dysfunction. Secrets are the foundation of denial; secrets from others or from ourselves. Secrets are the fuel for collusion, the enabling of addiction or abuse. Secrets are a source of fear and shame, they fuel the intergenerational family pathology.

Helen had been having suicidal fantasies since early adulthood. Now in her mid-thirties she began to develop elaborate images of the impact her death would have on those around her and how she would commit it. Her older brother to whom she seldom saw or spoke, called her late one evening and in a tearful discussion, she told him how she had been feeling and what stress she was under. He responded by telling her when she was nine years old, her mother had not died of cancer but overdosed on pills. He also told her that her mother's father, her grandfather, had witnessed his father hang himself when he was thirteen years old. The incidents and obsession with suicide had been in the family for several generations. Simply hearing the secret broken, understanding the intergenerational impact on her life was the first step for her recovery, not so much from the fantasies or suicidal ideations, as from the stress and terror. At least now she knew they had a source. Her mother's suicide had deeply affected her and at some level she had known the true circumstances of her mother's death

The secret is always known at a covert level and in a way that it can be reenacted. Family members always know what is going on - in their hearts, bodies, feelings, instincts. When given false information, a reality in one's head that doesn't match what is held inwardly, the true gut sense, it is natural to feel 'crazy' and disconnected, to not trust inner guides, instincts and feelings. How commonly has it been said, "I just knew or felt I should have left or done it differently." Many do not follow their wisdom because they have been damaged by the secret keeping. Not only self trust can be wounded but the ability to trust and feel secure with information and the sharing offered by others. One becomes overly skeptical or the flip side, naive.

Gloria repetitively got involved with dishonest men who conned her out of money or property. She had no natural distrust or warning signals. Whenever she was given a hard luck story by a current lover she accepted it at face value. Whenever she was told she would be paid back, she accepted it as true. She was easily conned, but she had been raised in a family where the children had always been told whatever would pacify them and virtually forced to accept all that was said at face value. Gloria's father ran a trucking business and several bars with gambling sessions in the back rooms. He had prostitutes working the bars and used the trucks for smuggling. Her repetition compulsion to be involved with men like her father and the 'no questions allowed' policy of her family set her up for a merry go round life of being used and abused.

These secrets sustained through dishonesty produce a lifestyle of stress and tension. Research has shown persons living with chronic stress over time can have the same reaction as persons experiencing trauma. Living in the stress of dishonesty is traumatic and may produce post trauma reactions and disorders.

The dishonesty of family brings about a dishonesty with self. The reality and impact of actions is distorted and minimized. Motivations, needs, behaviors or feelings are not understood nor are the long term effects of what is modeled.

John had been 'busted' for exposing himself. In a counseling session he mentioned his brother heard about his plight and wanted therapy as well. John's brother came in, spoke of having the same compulsion and wanted help. A few months into therapy they decided to do some family healing and invited their father in for a session. This was a courageous act for their father was very rigid, moralistic and judgmental. Half way into the session Dad fell to the floor sobbing and shared he had been exposing himself for over thirty years. This was not all coincidence. Dad had a secret and two sons were acting it out.

Several years ago I set up a therapy program for shoplifters who were referred to counseling by juvenile court. The parents met in a group setting once a month. As these parents became more honest and open they began to talk about their dishonesty. The most common specific incident of dishonesty mentioned by parents was their own history of shoplifting or other theft.

Much pathology is multigenerational. Even when not obvious the history usually surfaces with investigation. Shameful things are most denied, including, emotional or sexual affairs, sexual acting out, dishonesty, suicidal ideation and addictive disorders. In working with adolescents experiencing suicidal ideations or attempts, often the parents in family sessions begin discussing their own hopelessness and secret suicidal issues or those of other family members. Secrets cause much of the enmeshment discussed in principle number ten.

Joshua's brother overdosed on barbiturates when he was twenty years old, Joshua was twenty-six at the time. It impacted his life to the extent he made a career switch and began counseling troubled adolescents. Fifteen years later as he was sharing the pain of his brother's suicide and its effect on his life to a group of adolescents whose classmate had

recently suicided, Joshua remembered a long lost child-
hood incident.

He was about ten years old and heard the family car
running in the garage but the garage was closed. He got the
door open and in the car was his mother with her head
slumped over the wheel. He opened the car and helped her
into the house. The incident was never mentioned again nor
was it remembered until he was forty-one years old speaking
to the friends of the suicide victim. He realized his brother
acted out a suicide obsession and pattern that had been in
the family for several generations.

When he went home that night, at the table he told his
family of the realization. His eighteen year old daughter be-
gan sobbing and was eventually able to say, "I have been
planning on killing myself ever since I heard about the junior
high student who did kill herself. My boyfriend admitted he
got my best friend pregnant and I swore I would make him
and my friend pay by ending my life before the baby was born.
I know I won't do it now, but I need help."

How do we know to act out what we don't know? It is difficult to
live with someone who is suicidal without picking up their despair
and hopelessness. They say things reflecting the inner void, "Life is
no fun," "things never get better," "how can I go on?" It is difficult
to be around this over time without feeling and internalizing it.

The secrets are known because of the nature of communication.
We cannot not communicate and most communication takes place
at a covert level. Eighty percent of communication in a family is
nonverbal. What is said, what is left out or how it's said, all

communicate. The feelings and attitudes behind what is said say more than the words. The statement, "It is cold in the house," could be "The temperature is cold," "You didn't fix the furnace," "I need a sweater," or "I would like attention." We speak with our feelings, gestures, body posture, eyes, behaviors and attitudes. The nuances can speak louder than the words.

A family learns more by what is modeled than by what is said. Boundaries teach behavior. Healthy sexuality and honesty are taught by respect for boundary, the noticing and reactions to other's bodies, space, property and ideas. Communication is done through values, premises, rules, myths and beliefs.

A parent's rage at the world or belief, "you have to get them before they get you," sets up beliefs, feelings, and behaviors in the child. A parent's lust and seduction is felt and responded to by the child. In reacting to the energy points of the system we are pointed in directions and postures of behavior and lifestyles. Covert issues when not directly reacted to or acted out still set the tone and style for the operations and dynamics of the family. The denial of a particular problem or event sets the stage for a system operating on denial. The denial seeps into other areas of family functioning. An example may involve the denial of a parent's illness which becomes emotional denial in the family and may set up denial and repression of risk and loving openness. Members may no longer trust, they repress personal needs and ignore those of others. A true gift to family members is the open information of what is happening within, to and around the family and its members. Family secrets are also discussed in *Family Gatherings,* Family Secrets chapter.

The web of covert dynamics can easily become a trap where children of the system find themselves bound to destructive patterns of behavior and need.

Cathy, in a Lifeworks session realized some of the strands of her web. Included were her mom's self hate and distorted body image which Cathy carried out intact. Another strand of the web was mom's affair with a woman which Cathy reenacted in a similar period of her life, although her affair was with a man. A third strand was mom's sexual abuse as a child which affected Cathy's feelings about herself and her sexuality. The fourth strand leading to mom was her shaming and over criticizing which Cathy had internalized and recorded, playing it back over and over to herself. The fifth strand consisted of the emotional incest from dad where she took care of him and became enmeshed in his anger and his dependent postures. In fact she became the carrier of dad's unspoken passive/aggressive anger at mom. That strand of dad's deep anger and passive/aggressiveness left Cathy to fight dad's fight with mom. Another strand consists of four generations of women who had ran off with different men and left their families. Cathy had just been reenacting this by trying to run away from her family with a drug dealer. The last strand Cathy realized was dad's own lack of impulse control and addictiveness which became a pattern of impulsive/ destructive behaviors in Cathy's life including drugs, sex, and food. In understanding the web Cathy began to unravel and free herself.

CHAPTER 6

FIFTH PRINCIPLE
The Same Cause Can Produce Different Effects, The Same Effects Can Come From Different Causes

We are like snow flakes, each of us unique in our experiences, reactions, and offerings.

In an attempt to make sense and order of what is observed, repetitive efforts are made to link cause and effect and to produce a system telling us this cause will produce these effects or these effects come from this cause. The links made may contain an element of truth in that cause and effect have tendencies to flow from each other along particular paths. There are, however, too many variables to do a concise reading of the links. Accurate prediction of the effect of events in social, economic or even geophysical systems is impossible even though much energy and research has been produced attempting to do so. Nor can existing symptoms alone be used to map a trail back to a specific cause. It simply does not work to say because this happened or your family was such and such a way, you will be like this. Many books and articles on 'dysfunctional' families attempt to enforce a stereotype on the members of the families.

Mark was told his relationship with his fiancée was not healthy and he should separate from her because he came from a dysfunctional family, and healthy relationship was impossible until he resolved his issues. His choice was a continuation of the pathology of his parents. He ignored this advice and is still wonderfully in love with his fiancée who is now his wife of five years. The therapist who told him to break up is still trying to decide if she should enter her fourth marriage to a man who was recently placed on parole.

Humans are rich in complexities and possibilities. Each of us is unique in make up and reactions. A person may have been abandoned by a parent, the remaining parent may have been abusive or chemically dependent, but no one can say what the child will be like. Facts such as adaptability, role, birth order, gender, outside support, opportunities, thought process, confidants, biogenetics, brain chemistry, personality, character, spirituality and luck, good or bad, as well as other factors, too many to list, are all important. Problem areas and needs can be traced, but not all abuse victims are self destructive or have intimacy disorders and not all children of healthy families have healthy life styles.

People with similar life issues and scripts, common beliefs, learning styles and life postures can come from very disparate and differing systems. Twins raised in different families may have striking similarities. Twins raised in the same families, often have striking differences. In the book, *Broken Toys Broken Dreams* we listed one hundred possible traits of persons from low functioning families and for most of them we also added the opposite. The stimuli of family systems can produce either extreme, or any point of the continuum between. Powerful family stimulus often causes swings back and forth.

Gina was a diagnosed love addict and was told she must have been sexually bonded to her father. She read a book on love addiction and it told her specifically of the dynamics of her family. She tried to accept the principle but it just didn't fit and she felt more and more confused but afraid to switch therapists or dismiss the formulas of the 'experts.' After being hospitalized from severe weight loss from the stress of trying to resolve the puzzle, of trying to fit a piece into the wrong puzzle, she realized her love addiction was really an extension of her highly romanticized and imaginative childhood. The fairy tales and the solid loving connection of her parents made it difficult for her to accept the realities of relationship, and the peaks and valleys of ongoing intimacy. Her pattern was addictive but her family didn't fit the mold.

A person may be told they must be an incest victim because they have particular issues, possibly dissociation, intimacy disorders, isolation and sexual inhibition. These symptoms may also be reflected in a person who suffered from excess pressures to succeed. They may be a vicarious reaction to a parent's attitude and posture. The symptoms may be reactions to events outside of the family, an abusive marriage, or another trauma. In fact, there are myriads of situations and incidents producing these effects. In a similar vein, when a person reports having had incest memories they are often told what they must be like. They are scripted, so to speak, and told they are sexually dysfunctional, they are self destructive, they are withdrawn, they dissociate, when these symptoms are not necessarily present in all survivors of incest.

Brenda had been told on two different occasions she was an incest survivor. She had all the symptoms and behaviors indicating the particular trauma. She was also taught many incest and trauma survivors do not remember the incidents or experiences. Instead of relieved, Brenda felt devastated and 'crazy.' She knew her father as a loving man and could not imagine him doing such a thing. His patience with her mom and acceptance of mom's tremendous mood swings made him seem like a saint. She could not imagine any other family member or friend including her mom who seemed capable of doing such a thing to her. After her relationship with her family had been strained almost beyond repair the entire family scheduled a session. Brenda shared with her family what she had been told. She believed the family would be appalled and reject her for even considering such a thing. She was terrified it might be true but what she saw and experienced surprised her in a different way. Her mom who she had never been very close to got out of her chair and knelt before her, with both arms around Brenda's frightened body her mom said, "You were not incested by your father my dear, but I was by mine and your father has helped me heal my wounds slowly over time and I see now how many of my wounds have left scars on you."

The symptoms are merely earmarks or clues. When over interpreted and rigidified, false realities grow leading to dead end paths. Much of the discussion of reactions and symptoms to various situations and settings is unresearched and based only on personal experiences of the theory founder. Much researched data is based on a limited number of subjects and shows only tendencies, not linear projections.

Linking is an important aspect of self awareness and change. Responses and events need to be connected, behaviors to feelings,

feelings to processes, consequences to behaviors. The links allow understanding of the continuous processes of life and facilitate choice making. False links can set up false paths. Anger may be linked to a current relationship or past family pressure but it may be job related or rooted in a lost memory of a trauma event. It may also be a combination of events past and current that attach to minor irritations.

Symptoms have origins. Discovery and discussion of cause and effect can be accomplished without rigidity. Many have had few choices about events occurring around them or to them. One cannot *not* respond to these issues but frequently the link between the event and the response is lost. Perceiving the links between causes and effects allows the realization that self defeating behaviors are not about who we are but are about what has happened to us. This 'Linking Thinking' is an ongoing trend for instilling greater choice and less compulsive reaction. Healing the reality of ongoing destructive behavior requires linking the behavior in an ongoing way to the loss, hurt, trauma or modeling that set it up. While making these crucial therapeutic links it is helpful to keep in mind many of the effects are not from a single causal event but may have multiple sources. They spring not only from remembered or forgotten events but also from processes. These processes, ongoing stressors and repetitive patterns are generally more difficult to link to their responses. Living with chronic stress from covert repetitive double binding messages can cause similar effects to living with incidents of physical or sexual violence and assault.

Dan had been diagnosed with a mental illness. He had spent most his childhood and early adulthood in horrible double binds. As an adolescent he was regularly told he must get a job, but whenever he found a job his parents would ridicule his efforts and meager paycheck and sabotage his good feeling about what he was doing. Even as an adult he would check the 'want ads' after they would pressure him to find a job. When he found something, his parents would follow him to the interview and on his return, they would tell him what a horrible place that was, and he wouldn't want a job like that, or they didn't want a son of theirs doing that kind of work. Eventually all he did was sit in his rocking chair, listen to music with his earphones, watching TV with the sound off. The double binding had virtually immobilized him.

One person may respond to severe childhood neglect by entering the priesthood to care for needy children, another by having eleven children, another by becoming a narcissistic hoarder who lives alone and only for self.

The formulas do not work. There are no absolutes. Links must be made based on observed unique experience. Information and guidance can help make this link but only the individual can ultimately judge the application and accuracy of personal cause and effects. Resolving the ongoing destructive effects is done by linking them to their causes and maintaining the link through the healing process.

CHAPTER 7

SIXTH PRINCIPLE
Families Operate By Rules, Overt And Covert

Keep rules to a minimum, Expect basic courtesies,
Reach toward not away

Roots & Wings

Rules govern most areas of family functioning. Overt rules are not necessarily written or spoken, but clearly identifiable and usually easily articulated. Overt rules often cover issues such as discipline, economics, meals and meal times, religion, friends, curfews, dress, hair, language used, and conflict resolution. There are usually overt rules about sex, pregnancy, relationships, attitudes, education, gender and even emotional responses. Overt rules may or may not be healthy, they are often rigid but more easily broken because they are known. When the rule no longer makes sense or fits, decisions may be made to change or ignore it. Some overt rules have been present in families for generations and the reasons for the rule no longer apply.

Will's family had meal times at 4:45 every afternoon. If it wasn't served and eaten by 5:15 punishments were meted out or fights would break out. The reason for the rule was a great grandfather on the father's side had a job in a small town at the rail depot and the evening train arrived at 5:30. If he didn't eat by 5:15, he wouldn't be able to eat until much later. The rule stuck long after the reason for the rule no longer existed.

Rules are enforced through feedback. The difference in feedback may set up acting out or breaking the rules.

A very angry family strongly enforced a 'no hitting rule.' If someone did hit, they were so severely shamed and isolated they felt awful for a long period of time. Jim entered school where the rule was 'if you hit, you get detention.' A lot of his friends were in detention anyway so all his acting out took place in school, not at home where the anger was so intense. It took place in school because the feedback system was less severe, not that the rule was different or school the cause. When school personnel called the parents, they simply said, "It isn't our problem. He never behaves like that here. We don't allow it. It must be something wrong on your end."

Changing or breaking rules causes stress and discomfort. Many rules are held as tightly as rituals. Rules can offer security and meaning. Everyone needs to learn to play by the rules. They help us function with each other. Some rules however prevent functioning.

The most difficult rules to break are the covert ones. It's difficult to break a rule if we don't know it's a rule. The issues governed by overt rules may also have covert rules attached.

Harold's family rule was, 'everyone goes to church Sunday morning.' The covert rules however were, 'leaving early is OK, not paying attention is expected, criticizing the minister or service is required, Sunday mass attendance is all the spirituality we need and we go to show the neighbors we are a religious family.'

Rules can govern feelings. There are rules on anger, crying and sadness, there are rules about grieving, joy and fear. Oftentimes there is a time limit on the feeling itself. Some families will allow only a few minutes for joy and then it is removed, something will be said or done to spoil it. Crying is not tolerated since it makes one vulnerable and dependent. The tears may be teased or beaten out of the child to make the children less dependent on caregivers, to 'toughen up' the child. Sometimes a feeling is okay for one member of the family but not others. Possibly only dad or mom can get angry, but not the children. Sometimes one child is allowed temper tantrums but no one else is allowed any expression of anger.

Covert rules generally govern relationships; who talks to whom, who a particular child really connects to. There are covert rules about property, sex and drugs. Covert and overt rules often conflict giving double messages. An example is, 'don't do drugs,' but the modeled behavior is 'do drugs' because the parents are using nicotine or alcohol, or 'don't swear' but the members of the family do swear. In some families the rule may be drugs are not good, but medicating feelings is essential or is necessary for one or more people in the family. The feelings may be medicated with food or some other behavior rather than drugs.

Breaking rules is often done within the rule structure itself. Some families even have a rule that rules exist to be broken. Some of the rules, especially covert ones, likely to exist in a low functioning family are:

- Do not question.
- Do not notice.
- Do not feel.
- Do not talk.
- Be loyal only to the family.

- Stay the same.
- Be nice.
- Be good.
- Be compliant.
- Do not trust anyone but us.
- You have no choices.
- Do not take care of yourself.
- No one else will care or be involved.
- Do not make waves.
- Ignore absences.
- Do drugs.
- Medicate pain.
- Boys do not need affection.
- Boys are worth more.
- Boys need to be punished more.
- Girls need to be protected more.
- Girls need to be told no.
- Do not cry.
- Do not get angry.
- Do not mention problems.
- Do not get sick or be hurt.
- Getting sick or hurt is the only way of receiving attention.
- Do not acknowledge mistakes.
- Parents are always right.
- It's OK to hurt others but not yourself.
- It's OK to hurt yourself but not others.
- Do not get close to people outside the family.
- Do not get close to anyone.

- Do not trust anyone.
- Get yours at any cost but do not get caught.

Some families are shame based. The family members are caught in a process of increasing worthlessness and decreasing healthy dependency. The adult's shame experience is projected onto the children and the family practices rituals and enforces rules maintaining the sense of flaw, inadequacy, non-risk taking and self hate. These rules may spur efforts toward perfectionism to cover the shame but end up increasing it. Some of the rules governing a shame based system include:

- You must always do the right thing.
- Mistakes are not tolerated.
- You will not be told what the right thing is.
- Doing the right thing is impossible anyway.
- You must share success.
- Failures are blamed.
- There is not enough to go around.
- For you to get your needs met is selfish.
- Don't do what will hurt others, others are hurt quite easily.
- If you make a mistake there is something wrong with who you are not what you did.
- You must obey, fear and respect, but you cannot depend on anyone.
- For every good there is an equal bad.
- Don't feel too good because you'll just hurt more when it's gone.

Rules are revealed in the repetitions and patterns of family life. The feedback system will also indicate when rules are present.

Chuck's family maintained a covert rule about weight. He didn't realize the rule until he violated it. He had always been fifteen to twenty pounds over his 'ideal' weight and his family frequently commented on how healthy he looked. He began running and while training for a marathon he lost twenty pounds, the feedback from family members ranged from concern to abuse. They tried to feed or shame him back to weight. After an injury he gained weight, when he reached thirty pounds over ideal weight the family feedback turned on him again with comments about needing a diet or living too much of the 'good life'. The rule was 'to be healthy you need fifteen to twenty pounds of extra weight' - otherwise there is something wrong with you.

Breaking rules engenders guilt unless the rule is to break the rules. The rules are guides but many guide us away from our path. Rules must be weighed in context. They must be interpreted and the consequences of breaking rules needs to be noticed and linked to the rule breaking behavior.

Hilda's family had strict rules including one about calling parents on holidays. The parents never called the children however. While Hilda and her husband were in Jamaica over Easter she neglected to call. Her parents guilted and raged when she returned home for a visit. Hilda's subsequent shame and depression seemed unresolvable until she was able to connect it to the simple and trivial missed phone call. She had been hooked into a spiral of self recrimination based on an unreasonable and one sided expectation. A family rule had been broken and though her parents may have felt slighted, mostly they feared they were losing control of their daughter. The inconsequential rules were meaningful and important because they allowed the parents to maintain a sense of absolute authority over their children.

Healthy rules support self care, hygiene, rest, creativity and learning. Healthy rules value uniqueness, spontaneity, respect, and support.

The fewer rules the less energy is spent in enforcement and less rebellion and rule breaking occurs. Rules are often needed around safety issues but respect and care generally govern better than rules. When rules are flexible the compromising prevents breakages. When rules are rigid they are brittle and often weak. Rules and discipline are taught through modeling not enforcement. Many adults who do not keep rules spend great effort to enforce rules.

CHAPTER 8

SEVENTH PRINCIPLE
Individual Roles Maintain the Family system

Roles can give us a place so we have a place to give.

A family is a multifaceted, dynamic, changing organism. Family members at any given time have several roles facilitating the functioning and survival of the system. A family system can be a positive or a destructive life experience, the impact continuing through adulthood. A comedian recently stated that, "Coming from an alcoholic family is like having PMS all the time!" The stress of family is difficult to let go of as are the strengths. The roles played in family often shape our destiny.

The concept of roles is a fascinating aspect of family systems. Many functions we perform can be viewed in terms of role, including sexual, social, spiritual, recreational or work.

A role consists of patterns of behavior designed to allow or support family functioning. Many family roles depend more on a person's ability to adapt than on being smart, strong, good, bad or other personal attributes.

We often look at children and believe the successful child is in less pain than a non-successful child, and the successful child has more character. The success, overachieving or even underachieving may have to do more with adaptability and the assignment of role position than the particular attributes of the child.

Roles can be overlapping and multiple, they can change, reappear or be newly adopted. Roles have a lasting impact on our lives, a residual effect lingering long after the role has been left. Some roles are never left. There are several types of roles played out at various times and in different settings. Many of them have to do with the specific areas in where one operates.

Each level of society, Kessler calls them subsets, requires roles to maintain the level or subset. The individual develops roles to maintain self. These flow from our unique experience, personality, and self perception. There are roles regarding consumerism, health, self care, and identity. Another subset includes marriage and relationship, those involving spouse, friend, and partnership roles. They may include providing, maintenance, sharing, support, communication and sexuality. Then come family roles; parent, child, provider, learner, teacher, responsibility, roles concerned with needs, and roles to offer the family meaning and community. Neighborhood and community roles follow and they reflect involvement with community goals and maintenance. State and regional involvement also include roles. Here the level of involvement may primarily be political but could include education, consumer protection, or pressures for change. Cultural, societal, religious and national roles effect lifestyle, choices and values. Roles also exist based on our species and having to do with our planet. Conscientious planetary roles would include guardianship and carefulness about pollution, restricting the excess use of resources, recycling, working for the betterment and protection of life on the planet, or the maintenance of the beauty of the planet. Destructive postures toward the planet would be a form of offending role but may hide under the guise of 'developer' or 'visionary.' Roles seem to be primarily about behavior but attitude, ideas, beliefs, feelings, and settings are important in role functioning.

Many of the roles in the larger subsets regarding religion, society and planet are extensions of the roles learned as an integral part of the family system. A concern for justice and environmental respect, a gentleness towards life, a spiritual sense of gratitude and community is learned or often a reaction to something experienced or witnessed in family. A nurturing role may stem from a nurturing environment or one of neglect, it may be a reenactment or reaction.

Two women had belonged to a community recycling program. They both spent much of their life energy working for conservation and facilitating the recycling of waste products in the area. One came from a family where both parents and all the children were active in community projects, and the parents had been sponsoring a shelter for the homeless as well as running a sand and gravel business. The other came from a family of seven children. The father had left shortly after the birth of the youngest and mom spent much of her time hanging around the bar where she worked as a cocktail waitress.

The one constant in life is change, and as change occurs conditions and roles change. Low functioning systems set up low functioning roles. Some of the roles actually maintain the non-functioning aspects of the system. These low functioning roles limit choices and involve a loss of self relationship and esteem. They facilitate emotional denial and reality distortion, including enabling roles, offending roles and helpless victim postures. As systems become higher functioning the ability to adapt to the more functional system requires higher functioning roles. Clinging to the old roles and old system weaknesses in the new system sets up a rejection process. Functioning in or integrating into the healthier system is hindered while maintaining the old roles.

Addictions to money, work, power or sex can all stem from roles which play out the addictive activity or experience in some manner. The role sets up the addictive process. The little princess or prince role can charm dad or mom and begin a path of insatiable seduction and sexual acting out. The manipulator becomes hooked on control. The productive one becomes the work addict.

One person in the family may become compulsive about always looking good or making the systems look good, another works at being the genius or always trying to figure things out. Reinforcement for always looking good or doing the exciting, smart, or cool thing can set up roles as well as become addictive processes.

In the writings on role theory there has been a tendency to oversimplify and stereotype roles. It is often taught there are only four or five roles in a family and one particular role is lifelong. We have observed families as very complex and roles frequently shift or overlap.

Roles have a profound effect on the quality of life. Healing from the effects of unhealthy roles begins with making them real. It is essential to notice the role, to recognize and access the feelings and belief structures imposed on us by it.

Role theory is based largely on enmeshment. Enmeshment and covert roles can play a definitive part in family life. Enmeshed roles include extension roles, scripted roles, inappropriate bonding roles, taking care of the system's needs and role reversals. When the appropriate person in the system doesn't meet their role responsibilities, someone else moves in, usually a child, and takes over the responsibility. Some roles reflect enmeshment in the conflicts, denial and mythology of other individual members, their relationships or the system itself. The resulting roles can damage development. Becoming enmeshed in the losses, expectations, and destructiveness of others sets up a loss of spirit and individuality.

Roles are difficult to give up or change because they involve self concept, beliefs, feelings and habits. They involve how we view ourselves, the world, premises about life, and mythology about self and family. To change roles, basic premises and beliefs must be reevaluated. Roles are based on beliefs and messages received in various systems; nuclear family, work, social relationships, school and community. The roles become woven into our external and internal systems like crocheting. Changing or dealing with a particular role is like changing a stitch in the middle of a piece of crocheting. Real change involves unraveling the basic structure and reworking it. It involves looking at how other roles have become interrelated and understanding the system where they evolved and the needs they met.

Because roles are crucial to survival and functioning in family, the role is easily confused with identity. Unconscious transference of identity to the role can set up an over identification with the role. Role offers place, purpose, value, self definition, and a style of relationship functioning. False identity comes from over identifying with the role as clown, one can be the victim, addict, offender or hero. Section II of *Family Matters,* covers role theory in more depth.

CHAPTER 9

EIGHTH PRINCIPLE
Family Is A System Of Dynamic Homeostasis, Change With Resistance

Life is a flowing river of process and change.
Reflections

The concept of dynamic homeostasis is similar to an ice floe moving but frozen in time. Family is a social system and all social systems change but there is a resistance to the change, a tendency for things to remain the same or go back to being the same. Once again relying on the mobile image, the mobile may be symmetrical and balanced or off balance, flat and lacking form. Providing tension or weight to one part of the mobile may give it motion, energy, or substance, but walk away for a while, and the mobile will soon return to its original form, whether it was off balance or in balance.

Families and people are similar. Families may come together or seek help in crisis, but when the crisis is over or the help ends, the family generally gravitates back to the structure of the old system. Conflict can even be a part of the homeostasis. Family feuds with other families, such as the 'Hatfields' and 'McCoys' can be a part of the on going structure of the family. Homeostasis involves a resistance to change even when change is inevitable. Change can cause power struggles and stress within the system. Parents who attempt to over control and keep children and family in a particular posture or developmental stage set up the acting out response of the child.

This is especially true of adolescents who when overcontrolled, tend to fire parents who don't retire.

The concept of change and resistance is often reflected in helping relationships. Helpers who need to help others in order to avoid looking at themselves find their need to help runs into the other's need to stay the same, their resistance to change. This causes a collusion of defenses, the defenses of each party collide and escalate thereby enabling both postures. The helpers need to help intensifies and subsequently the resistance to help increases. The ensuing power struggle frustrates both sides.

This principle is a common lesson for addicts. Many alcoholics have learned there is no recovery as an event, it is a lifelong process consisting of making changes in an ongoing way. There is a tendency to believe one can make the big change, find a fix, go to a workshop and alter our lifestyle and the alteration will remain forever. The only way change lasts is to keep the change alive, to do the changing each day. To move in a new direction, the movement in a direction must be ongoing. The energy and healthy tension of the change must become a part of daily life. There are no cures, only processes maintained through a new way of living. Changes in behavior and postures towards life, thinking and feeling can be profound and make healthy living easier. New behavior must accompany deep changes in thoughts and attitudes or the old beliefs and feelings resurface. Healing is journey and process, not goal or destination.

ENTROPY

In a family system the dynamics of entropy operate in a dual state of change and resistance to change. Entropy is a theory of movement toward chaos with random displacements and attachments. Entropy had been discovered as a principle of physics and observed in molecular biochemistry research but parents of adolescents had already identified it. Entropy tells us change is absolute, essential and uncontrollable.

A recently developing complexity/chaos theory indicates the more elements involved in a system, the change and development of the system becomes less predictable and the organization of the system is more difficult. When human thought, feelings and behaviors are involved, the complexity/chaos factor is high.

As society becomes more complex with population increases, movement and diversity, information and technological changes, greater difficulty exists in managing and predicting economic, legal, social and ecological issues. Our societal chaos stems in large part from our growing complexity. We are also witnessing an increase in the complexity of family relationships; needs, time schedules, stressors, demands, ownership, maintenance, roles, distance, awareness, legal and economic issues. Families are more complex and chaotic. Thus the tension between the need for stable homeostatic maintenance and the need to grow and adapt to the evolving cultural and familial alterations is also escalating. This tension is a source of increased conflict and stress perpetuating and intensifying the dual posture to change and to stay the same.

Social systems, including families have a powerful static drive, great energy is placed into maintaining the structure, rules, and overall family dynamics. This is a losing battle but an important one that must be waged without excess rigidity and fear, for change will come anyway. Excess rigidity may cause fissures and even chasms into the value of the system, or the family may be crushed. The fear of change may cause panic and futile attempts to overcontrol or deny the changes. Rigidity causes elements of change to be dismissed as no longer part of the system.

Change in the system allows the family to adapt to change outside the family; the changes in world, culture, climate, economics, stress, values, etc. Change also allows the growing of family toward a deeper quality and sense of value and meaning. When external change is too great and too rapid for the culture or family to assimilate, the process is a traumatic loss of connection and meaning. The cultural genocide of Native North Americans or Australian Aboriginals is an example of change where the culture is lost. The resulting chaos is seen in depression, suicide rate and rampant alcoholism.

The attempts to maintain and resist change have the quality of preserving. Constancy is the fertility of positive growth. The static system is the spark for change just as many of the changes gradually spiral into the hold of static value. The premises and structure we go about conserving sometimes are the revolutionary and rebellious notions of past generations.

The liberal cannot liberate without the conservative effort to conserve. The one needs the other and both are of value. The conflict of the two postures is the tension, often generational, requiring both dynamic appreciation of the static as well as static support of growth toward positive dynamics.

The entropy is found in the latter, a growth toward the chaotic. The physical laws of science can't seem to prevent the disorganization of nature's systems be they complex molecules or the galaxies.

Given the chaos of the physical universe, what chance do we have to maintain the organization of our simple families - it seems little to none. The harder we try the greater is our acceleration into chaos. As families move toward chaos, we may attempt to control the flow or enjoy the rapids, but damming the rivers of change produces flood and destruction. Family chaos is not necessarily the turbulence of devastation but rather a bending, breaking and stretching of patterns - roles, rules, premises, tradition and style, a dissolving of organization into a broth with its own flavor.

In families, as in nature and society, the drift is toward breaking the set laws. The laws of gravity are fixed and yet this sentence is written while traveling five miles above the ground. Life is constantly breaking the physical laws that would constrain or refrain it.

Cultures are constantly faced with members who break the laws. Many of these law breaking rebellious members of society are punished to prevent a societal fall into a lower value system of chaos but many eventually become an essential part of the culture enhancing it toward greater quality and survival. This is true in government and politics but even more so in the arts and sciences. In family this rebellion eventually can be incorporated as family strength and creativity.

The limits are tested and broken, the mold is altered, and the system emerges with a new value and way of functioning. This parallel is also repeated individually when one breaks the older patterns of their lives to discover potential and fulfillment. The individual process toward greater life quality may be the forerunner and scout for the family to follow. At this juncture fracturing may occur, more chaos, but even the fracturing can be a test of the values and quality where a blend of static and dynamic may appear. Even though the new is dismissed it impacts systems and what is dismissed is still part of the system just as it operates primarily in the old system paradigms and dynamics.

Embracing the new without discarding the old is a chaotic struggle but can evolve into patterns of movement toward fulfillment. The breakdown, brokenness and trauma allow reorganization and new direction. Robert Pirsig maintains "life is a migration of static patterns toward a dynamic quality." The chaos and trauma causing the disorganization allow an expansion of boundary, deeper meaning and value, or as Jean Huston calls it, "a soul awakening."

The progress of humanity is like climbing a stairway toward a higher good, each step contradicts the existing norms, the upward motion requires greater effort. The step up must rest on something solid and level to maintain the offering, if not the step descends again to the level where it began.

A family with effort raises itself to a higher value but the rise must be protected by the landing, the base of conserving. The protection for dynamic value is the static resistance. As the reevaluations become the rules, resistance reasserts itself. An oscillation effect appears; reaction, counter reaction and reaction. The growth is similar to the ascension of a spiral staircase winding around itself, covering all points of the circle while moving toward a higher place.

Personal change and expansion of awareness comes with the courage of moving through life's losses and changes and brings about the ascension of family awareness. The family however is like a long snake with the tail wiggling somewhere behind and below. The changes may not seem to effect each member of a family but what effects one effects all and the effects are multigenerational.

The tendency toward chaos is the constant of change. Change always involves loss and gain, in the exchange is the chaos, the evolution of the organism. Change does not follow a particular mold or path. The stairway might look like a neurotic roller coaster.

The tendency to violate existing law and structure is not evenly balanced with the tendency to retain the stasis and existing laws. At times one or the other dominates. The resulting chaos can be destructive in the overconserving system not equipped to cope with internal natural growth or the external changes and pressures. The over conserving element also intensifies the rebellious forces to the extent the dynamic direction may become destructive. When change occurs, with little regard for conserving, the positives of change are neither tested nor reflected upon, the change then rests on shaky ground and the unbridled fluctuation tends toward destructive chaos. It is past gain that we conserve. Without energy invested in conserving, gains are not maintained. The resultant looseness produces random disconnection. Tradition and rituals and other guides and sources of meaning are absent or quickly lost.

The movement toward chaos - dynamic change, facilitates growth, the maintenance of homeostasis facilitates perseverance. Growth and perseverance are important and symbiotic qualities resting on each other but also conflicting with each other. The friction can be reduced with communication and sensitivity but the rub is still present.

Chaos, the disorganization of the social system rules and patterns is not a true chaos but a part of a reorganization incorporating the differences and accommodating the change. The process of reorganization out of the chaotic change can be the source of energy in the system. The chaos cannot be mapped yet follows its own course, in balanced systems the course is from chaos to quality.

Without static quality the family will not last, without dynamic quality the family cannot grow and adapt, both are needed.

Much of this is acted out in the colloquial generation gap. The awareness of the need for both pressures, respect for conserving as well as respect for changing bridges this gap. The sons and daughters who test and stress but still value and carry tradition while charting new courses carry the family to its new heights. When conserving becomes over control, the next generation is set up to over react and vacates the family or is forced out. This stress is a source of energy but easily becomes the distress found in so many unhappy and disconnected families.

CHAPTER 10

NINTH PRINCIPLE
Families Function Within Boundaries: Personal, Structural And System

Boundaries are a construct of identity. We cannot set our limits until we know our limits. We cannot know our limits until we know ourselves. Once we know ourselves we have our limits.

Reflections

Boundaries are bridges not walls. Families have three basic kinds of boundaries providing structure and identities. There are *system* boundaries of the family as a whole, *personal* boundaries of each member within the system, and *structural* boundaries forming the internal structure of the system .

SYSTEM BOUNDARIES

In a low functioning family the boundaries are either under formed or nonexistent on one hand, or rigid and non-permeable on the other. An alcoholic family usually has rigid boundaries to maintain. Information about the disease of alcoholism does not enter the family, it may destroy the system. If information about the effects of the alcoholism is spread outside the family, it too may destroy the system. Violent families often have rigid boundaries for similar reasons, once information of the violence gets out, the system is threatened. No one is allowed to talk about family issues and reality.

Leaving a family with rigid boundaries can be very difficult. Boundaries effect how people enter and leave the system. Many rigid systems allow little outside contact into the family. Rigid systems hold members in a tight grip.

Jane was being sexually molested by her father. She was not allowed to have any friends at the house, nor were her brothers and sisters. Her parents had little social contact except for rare occasional outings. The family home seemed to have a wall around it, people knew not to approach. Jane tried once to tell her mother and her mother just glazed over and walked away. Jane knew then she must not tell anyone. She now knows the same thing was happening to her sisters but they couldn't even talk about it with each other. The boundaries in the family were not just around the house, the wall was around each person living in the house. Janet broke the silence and the ensuing anger and chaos eventually became a healing process for her siblings.

Systems with weak boundaries provide little sense of belonging, little unity or family pride. Insecurity and acting out flow from the absence of as well as rigidity of boundary. Boundaries define the system from which the members of the system find definition of self. An open door policy with the outside world is healthy but chaos results from too much external intrusion and confusion.

Dan was raised in Wadena, Minnesota and found a job in California in the computer industry. He was there for eighteen months but did not feel right. He came back home and bought a small house two blocks from his parents and went on unemployment. He spent his mornings drinking coffee with mom, and his evenings drinking beer at the same bar his father frequented. Eight years later after a uncompleted suicide attempt, with the help of counseling he began to break the hold of the family and the town on his life.

Overly loose boundaries can leave children living in an unpredictable and unsafe setting. In a home where illegal activities take place, where drug dealing or gambling is a regular way of life, a child never knows who will be there and whom they can or cannot trust. In a family where relatives or others come and go, sometimes staying for long periods of time, a child does not know who they can get close to, who has authority, or how long anyone will be around. In single parent families where the parent has numerous partners or has short term serial monogamous partners, it is difficult for a child to know who to rely on and issues of trust and discipline become confusing.

System Boundaries effect the flow of persons and information in and out of the family. In mechanical systems boundaries are rigid and can be changed by adding, subtracting or altering parts. In social systems the boundaries must be fluid and permeable since change and openness is a part of the system. Social systems are like living organisms flowing and growing, discovering and multiplying. Permeability of boundaries means some openness and some closeness. Information and people must be able to pass through, enter and leave, filtered by the unique experience and need of each individual family member.

Often when a system appears to have a rigid boundary system, to be a very closed, tight knit family, overtly the family is enmeshed, but covertly the system is detached with individuals not really feeling connected or able to exhibit real caring. When the system is overtly boundariless with everyone disengaged, the underlying system may exhibit a deep emotional bond to the point of enmeshment in each other's reality and feelings. Any model for System Boundaries must take into account the covert system as well as the overt. Connecting, belonging, and loyalty have many faces and come in many forms, some healthy, some unhealthy.

Roy grew up in a family where he did not feel he belonged. His parents fought pretty much all of the time and seemed to hold very little interest in Roy's life. Roy had a surrogate family however. He had a friend his own age and when his friend wasn't home he would simply hang around the family. Even when the family wasn't home he would walk in and watch TV until they got back. He had dinner with them, watched television with them, he prayed with them, he frequently did his homework there. He also had another friend. When visiting this friend, he would knock on the door and the door would open a little bit, and he would say, "Can John come out?" He was told to wait, and the door closed. He never got a foot in the foyer. He and John were friends, but John wasn't very talkative. Eventually it came out that John came from a very hurtful violent family and had an older brother living in the basement whom Roy had never even met.

PERSONAL BOUNDARIES

Personal boundaries are those aspects of identity defining limits and uniqueness. These boundaries, when healthy, produce healthy choices and balanced lifestyle. Unhealthy boundaries follow violence, the violation of one's body, rights, needs, space, sexuality, spirit, ideas and creativity. Abuse is a broad term for these violations.

Sherri related that she was twenty-six years old before she realized she had the right to say no to whatever anyone wanted from her if they dated or befriended her. She had been used sexually and financially by people she had no interest in but somehow felt she owed them. Sherri found it very difficult to take care of herself and frequently went on eating binges, gaining weight and then would fast or do a fad diet to lose weight. She eventually connected her absence of personal boundaries and absence of self care to the constant intrusions, molestation, and physical abuse she endured as a child growing up in a family of raging addicts.

Abuse is distinguished into categories and usually differentiated by physical, sexual, emotional, intellectual and spiritual. This is done to help us recognize the difference in the event, response, recovery and healing needs. It is also done because of the differentiation in boundary discussion between physical, sexual, emotional, intellectual and spiritual. It has been theorized if violence and abuse are violations of boundaries, then the lines must be clear between the types of abuse if ther are different types of boundaries. On closer examination this theory falls short of the truth and the focus on a particular type of abuse may prevent an integrated and full recovery process. Boundaries are not really separable and discussion of differences in sexual, physical and spiritual boundaries fails to recognize the wholeness of the human experience and the integration of human beings. Paul Turnier once said, "The mystery of human existence eludes us because we do not look at the whole person."

Boundaries cannot be broken down by using terms such as external and internal, physical or sexual, emotional or intellectual. Setting limits is seen as a primary boundary building exercise and limits are usually seen as external. Limits, however, are internal as well as external. *We cannot set limits until we know our limits and we cannot know our limits until we know ourselves. Once we know ourselves we have our limits. Boundaries are a construct of identity.* Building identity builds boundaries that are gentle, resilient, respectful and strong. Setting external boundaries sets up a brittle, artificial, rigid and fragile superstructure.

A limit is knowing what one can tolerate, handle, accept and process. These tell how close we feel comfortable to another, how much work can be taken on, how much food is healthy and so on. These limits are acquired in the journey of self awareness and identity and are part of self care inherent in healing. (See more on Identity Building and Self Esteem in *Family Gatherings.*) More often than not the real hurt or violation of abuse does not happen externally, rather it is internal, thus the healing must takes place internally as well. Bodies heal, our property is repaired or replaced, but the damage to our souls, self esteem, and thought process takes more time and nurturing support to heal. We are beings with our bodies, spirituality, sexuality, thoughts and feelings all integrated and interactive.

Certain forms of boundary violations have differing effects. The violence is manifest in a variety of responses. The discussion of the violations and a linking to the possible response is discussed in detail in *Broken Toys Broken Dreams,* BRAT Publishing, 1990. The differentiation in abuse is still in large part, artificial. All abuse is sexual, all abuse is spiritual, all abuse is physical, intellectual and emotional, requiring healing in all of the above. Violence produces reactions in each area. Each response seeks a link to the cause and demands expression until debriefed.

All aspects of our being, sexuality and spirituality are interwoven, a tear in the fabric of one always requires mending in the other. Sexuality is a core of identity, spirituality is the core of existence, our being - we cannot separate who we are from that we are. Identity flows from being, body and spirit are one. Feelings, thoughts and physical being are a tapestry of personality, creativity and the manifestation of character and values. Damage from abuse is not compartmentalized. The effect echoes into each aspect of our lives and personhood. Abuse can rupture the spiritual core of our being and the broken spirit becomes fertile ground for addiction.

The big book of AA says alcohol is but a symptom. It is a symptom of spiritual bankruptcy. The disease of addiction effects physical well being, thoughts, sexuality and emotions. It destroys the ability to notice, form values and find meaning. The addiction is often a symptom of abuse. The abuse is trauma, a threat to survival and the fracturing of wholeness.

If the trauma is sexual or physical, emotional or intellectual, neglect or abandonment, each aspect is damaged and rendered more vulnerable to subsequent hurt. Healing must take place on all levels. When a child is abused physically, it damages their identity, the relationship with their body, and themselves as men and women. Physical healing from physical abuse must be accompanied by a restoration of the spirit, trust and noticing; a healing of gender identity, Manness and Womaness; emotional debriefing and grieving; awareness and intellectual sorting out, sense and meaning applied; realistic assessments made of possibilities of recurrence, the personal responses to the trauma, and the world we live in.

The relationship with oneself as a man or woman is the core of sexuality. Neglect or any form of abuse damages this relationship. It sets up self neglect and leaves deep emotional scars. All abuse is physical abuse, emotional abuse, intellectual abuse, spiritual abuse and sexual abuse, all healing and recovery must also incorporate each of the above.

Bill and Sara were brother and sister. Both were severely neglected by parents who were virtually never around, or if they were around, were so obsessed and involved with each other Bill and Sara were ignored. Bill medicated his neglect with self touch and masturbation. At an early age he was into pornography and fantasy. Sara medicated with food. She hoarded food and binged constantly. Both felt a great deal of shame, and both neglected themselves in severe ways. By the time they reached their mid-thirties they suffered from serious effects of their self neglect. The neglect was impossible for them to change until they made real how they had been neglected. Nothing changes until it becomes real. Understanding the soil in which their addictive behaviors took root helped them work a recovery program without the constant stress and relapse episodes.

STRUCTURAL BOUNDARIES

The structural boundaries are the boundaries within the system. The separateness and togetherness, distance and closeness of the family members are reflected in these boundaries. Again permeability is important. Structural boundaries define the limits of family relationship.

Although marriage is often defined in terms of 'union' with ceremonial phrases of 'flesh unto flesh' and 'becoming one' a blend of sharing and togetherness with separateness and individual ego is essential. One must keep their unique interests, creativity, productivity and connections. Emotional, physical and financial sharing need not lessen individuality, the ability to invest in self, maintain separate interests and productivity. A healthy individual has a better change for healthy relationship.

Healthy boundaries between adults and children involve the availability of adult support and nurturing without hovering or over intrusive postures. There are important boundaries between adults and children concerning sexuality, privacy of thoughts and feelings as well as time. Parents who over schedule children leave little time for exploration and development. Children are not in the system to fulfill the adults affectional or sexual needs, to give parents lives meaning, to fill in for what the parent failed to do or to be like the parent. Children own themselves, their bodies, ideas, freedom, choices, feelings, space and property just as adults do.

The boundary between the siblings or other dependents in the system is also important. Siblings have a well defined sense of boundary in healthy systems. They do not sexually intrude or physically violate to any great degree. This changes when the system is low functioning, abusive or neglectful. When sexual acting out, severe repression, sexual abuse or severe neglect is occurring elsewhere in the family the children are more likely to act out with each other. Within a physically abusive system siblings will likely physically abuse each other.

Most sibling anger arises from boundary violations. A child leaves a chair to get something and another sits in it. When the first child reappears to claim the chair, there may be an eruption. A sibling wears another's new sweater without asking - another eruption.

Boundaries are taught by boundaries modeled. When parents or caregivers exhibit healthy relationship and personal boundaries, children tend to adopt the same. When a parent cannot protect oneself, is always giving up emotionally, physically or with property, the result is boundary dysfunction. When a parent protects their own rights and property, refusing to be run over by others in or out of the system, the boundaries are more likely to be healthy all around. From healthy boundary true acts of kindness and spirituality flow. Giving need not be a symptom of poor boundaries, but a flowing of generosity when there is a choice. Boundaries offer choices and respect each other.

Parents can set limits on time, energy, finances, tools, toys, work and other activities. These modeled boundaries may engender complaint, but teach others how to take care of themselves.

Often the absence of boundary or identity sets up enmeshment. The enmeshment may breed resentment and build walls. Bonding and enmeshment issues are covered in the next principle.

CHAPTER 11

TENTH PRINCIPLE
Families Are Held Together Through Bonding -
Inappropriate Bonding Sets Up Enmeshment

Our relationships reflect our connection to creation.
Reflections

Early relationships are survival bonds, when early attachments are damaged the harm is reflected in subsequent relationships. The components of family are the relationship between family members and these relationships have a quality called a bond. A bond is the energy of the attachment, the emotional, legal and biological connection. Each bond is unique and varies over time. In infancy and early childhood the attachment bond is equal to survival.

We are social creatures, our life is about relationships, attachments. The prolonged attachment to survival figures enables humans to develop deeper bonding and have more time to learn. Early attachments effect future ones. When these early bonds are damaged, intimacy and future attachments are often a struggle.

Relationship with self flows from earliest bonding and is of great importance in determining well being as well as the ability to form healthy bonds with others.

The relationship with self and others is learned not just in one's relationship with parents or other care givers, but also in their relationship with each other, the modeled relationships of those around.

Intimacy is learned less by having parents be intimate with children than by children seeing it in the parent's adult relationships.

A frail child born of a strong marriage entered school and discovered for the first time he was different. As an infant he struggled to gain weight, his parents were told his heart was weak and they protected him in the folding of their own hearts. He was happy, cared for and playful, until he started school. For the next eighteen years he was teased mercilessly, called a nerd, sissy, mama's boy and wimp. He received good grades but was afraid to do any better because he knew he would be more noticed and teased. He spoke not a word to his parents of his pain but he always knew he would be safe with them and they loved him even though he was weak. Even the girls picked on him, except one.

She never spoke to him for she too was picked on and quite plain which was not okay for girls to be. This boy noticed her looking at him and even saw an occasional smile as if they shared a secret. He didn't know what the secret was but it gave him a warm glow inside, sort of like when he was between his mom and dad with his hands each in one of theirs and he could feel that warm glow flowing right through him in both directions.

The girl was still there the last year of high school but she had changed - kind of like these people who get makeovers on TV and become glamorous. She was glamorous which for some reason made him sad for he was still a 'nerd.' She was also still aloof, he noticed she had little time for all the boys and girls who teased her before but were now a little awed.

On the day before the last of day school, she approached the boy and said if you don't ask me out now you may never see me again. He stammered and said, "Sure, well, if you want to or I mean well, I will." They went out on a shy, silent date and walked under a June full moon. The first of many that summer. They attended different colleges that fall and maintained a magnificent poetic correspondence, each letter a Pulitzer Prize candidate full of passion and sensitivity. They married and worked hard through graduate school. They now have a child who walks between them and somehow notices a warm glow coming from both directions. They are both physicians specializing in bone marrow transplants and leading the research in the field. But more importantly they have a love story that grows and deepens each day. Where there is love there is always hope.

Since early bonds are survival issues, the inconsistency or absence of such bonding, or the abuse of the bond is a threat to survival, a trauma. Insecure or broken bonds create stress and fear. Children with poor bonding to survival figures are set up for dependency problems and bonding disorders. These include relationship problems and addiction, these are dependency issues. This early trauma may set up destructive reverberations throughout one's life. Insecurity, inappropriate relationships, using or offending, shame and fear based acting out frequently stem from the trauma of damaged survival bonds.

Abandonment is the withdrawal or absence of connection or availability from those to whom we have an emotional, nurturing and protecting commitment to, or a financial or legal obligation toward. The abandonment breaks off relationship in some manner, but it also damages the self relationship of the abandoned. This fractured identity and the frequently repressed feelings of abandonment are the cause of subsequent themes of abandonment in future relationships.

Chris was two years old when her father drove off for the last time and abandoned his family. When she was sixteen she talked of her boyfriend who would drop her off at home from a date, she wouldn't get out of the car. In fact she would take his keys and sit on them. He eventually learned to carry two sets of keys. For some reason every time he drove off, she had this panic, this fear she would never see him again. Chris didn't understand until her mother in a therapy session told of how she stood at the steps when her father drove off. She had repressed the memory, but it had set her up to fear abandonment and to cling on to relationships so tight sometimes she smothered the flame of the relationship.

Repetitive abandonments are more difficult to grieve and resolve. Neglect is a term used for a process of ongoing abandonment, the repetitive lack of involvement or availability of caregivers.

The child used by caregivers to meet the needs of the caregiver is also abandoned but the appearance may be of a close bond. Adult intimacy failure and repeated relationship disappointments can set up a process of adult over bonding with children. This is a reversal of roles, the child is being used to meet the needs of the parent. The needs may be emotional, affectional, physical, or sexual, for attention, meaning or control but the effect is similar. The repetitive using of a child for adult needs produces two primary reactions in the child.

Firstly the child survives the using or even thrives on it by accepting the fantasy of the parental love and the parental connection being for their own good. The relationship with the parent is based on the belief *my parent is there for me and I am special, rather then the reality that I must be there for the parent and I am being used.*

The second dynamic is an internal one, the child deeply senses being used and in combating feelings of overwhelm or smothering becomes more and more defended and internally defiant.

Upon leaving the family these two effects are played out by the now grown child by repetitively entering relationships where one partner is using the other, entering relationships where the anger of the past is manifested while maintaining a mythological view of the relationship, living out a bond of myth and fantasy. It matters little what type of relationship or fantasy is involved however since the inner defendedness prevents accepting or sharing true intimacy and vulnerability. A defiant counterdependence develops sabotaging the efforts for connection.

How common it is for a parent who is isolated and alone, who needs affection and attention to turn to the child and under the guise of giving is really taking. This dynamic of emotional incest is common in families. Follow a family down the sidewalk and watch for the real bonding and attentive connections. How often is one parent with one child, the other with another child? Commonly in this scene will be a lost and unbonded child, forever feeling left out and hanging around the periphery of life's dynamic.

Brandon's sister was daddy's little girl, who felt protective of daddy even after daddy physically battered her and her mom. She later married a batterer who holds her in a hostage relationship. Brandon's older brother was mom's little boy, he has been in relationship after relationship and continually feels used and smothered. Brandon however didn't feel like he belonged in the family. He would fantasize another family would take him away, that he would be their favorite. As an adult, Brandon kept getting into relationships he was interested in, and then bringing the person around to meet other people, and backing away waiting for the rejection to happen and for him to feel lost again. He had never closed the chapter on his orphan feelings in childhood, and kept setting himself up to feel like an orphan and to be left out.

Another inappropriate family bond stems from abuse. The child who is put down, judged harshly, beaten or molested frequently bonds with the offender. The offending pattern is an enslavement process where the victim loses power, choice and freedom. The beaten spouse in a battering relationship does not stay because they enjoy the abuse but is rendered helpless and bound by its repetition. Children as well, bond to survival figures even absent and abusive ones.

Occasionally a child will be double bonded, having to be a 'source' for both parents, living out both parents dreams and being on both sides. This is a devastating posture to be in for it causes a life of confusion - 'with the fusion' of two opposing realities. The over bonded child usually cannot bond in adult relationships but frequently sets up the same system by over bonding with their own children.

Overprotection is emotional incest under an assumed name, the protection being a projection of the parent's needs and fears. Some parents who as children were neglected smother their children with their own fears and needs in an attempt to stop the pattern of neglect.

Over bonding, covertly or overtly sets up enmeshment. One can no longer sort out their personal needs, dreams, wants, feelings or issues from those of the parent.

Scripting children involves using the survival bond for control and self gratification. Parents have historically projected so much of their own turmoil, guilt, and life struggles on their children the possibility of growth in child protection and parenting skills has been thwarted. If what befalls a child is felt like it is happening to the parent, the child gets little support or protection since the adult focus is on the adult. If what befalls a child occurs because of the parent's sin and is punishment for the parent's life indulgences, the child again goes unprotected and unnoticed as a separate entity.

For more information on emotional incest and family bonding issues see *Broken Toys Broken Dreams,* Chapter 10, 'Oedipus Wrecks and Electra Lights' and the section of Bonded Roles in Section II of this book.

Healthy family bonding begins when two adults with healthy identity are willing to commit to maintaining a primary friendship with each other. Children do better in a system of benign neglect with parental availability and the primary parental involvement in the marital relationship than in a system over focusing on children. In single parent families the parent must be available to children while meeting their own needs in adult relationships.

The bond between parents is the foundation of family, the bond between parents and children is the foundation for survival. Loyalty, love, protection and attention are not limited qualities needing to be rationed but can flow in abundance and wash through the family into community and future generations.

Sibling bonds are also important. These are generally the longest relationships we have in our lifetime, often reflecting the bond of the parent's relationship. Sibling anger covers stored pain and acts out marital discord.

Bonds not encouraging or respecting boundaries become enmeshment. Bonds to persons who hold a reservoir of hidden past, pathology and emotions set us up to sink into their reservoir and eventually leave having soaked up so much of what is not about our life or reality.

Enmeshment describes the inability to individuate, the absence of autonomy. It is the acting out of what is denied. Enmeshment is partially described in Principle number four. Enmeshment is the carrying of attitudes, behaviors, beliefs, labels, aspirations, frustrations, acting out, fears, angers, shame, guilt, postures or needs not truly belonging in our life and hindering our life processes.

Enmeshment stems from:

- Inappropriate bonding: over connecting, hovering, 'sticky' and 'using' parental style. A child is overwhelmed by the parent's expectations and projections. The ability to risk is lost in a pattern of anxiety and reactiveness.
- Over involvement in another's life, needs, feelings: developing a partnership or best buddy role with a child or the child becoming the caretaker or tool for an impaired parent. The survival bond between the child and parent or other survival figure evaporates the sense of separateness.

- Covert feelings and acting out in the system: adults who repress feelings and deny behaviors set up the children to act them out. Children sense the feelings and behaviors and make sense of what they intuit by experiencing the feelings and behaviors as their own.

- Absence of boundary sense: intrusive or prying parenting, no privacy allowed, inappropriate sharing with the child, assuming one knows more of the child's reality than the child. Parents can use their authoritative presence and experience to mold or control the child's reality often distorting and diminishing the child's uniqueness.

- Survival needs: a child learns 'to read' the feelings, signs, attitudes, fears and tension in erratic, unstable or addicted adults who may turn violent, abandon or 'split' unless the child reacts to what they read; gradually the child is enmeshed in and acting out what is read.

When Charles would come home from school his radar would go on and his antennae would go up. He would begin to notice things; the mood, the ambiance, he would notice the car, and how it was parked. He would notice if dad was home and if dad was tense or if mom was depressed, or sad, or packing, or preparing to leave, or if dad was drinking. He would notice if they were about to fight, or had been fighting or were fighting, and he always reacted to what he noticed. He would try to mediate the fights, he would try to patch things up, he would try to help his mom cheer up, or talk his dad out of the tensions or to not drink. Charles gradually developed the skill of noticing other people, what they needed and what they felt, but he never developed the skill to notice what he needed and what he felt. Gradually he felt a resentment in his life because he was always doing for others when no one would do for him, including him.

- Guilt disguised as love: parents who are wonderful, 'saint mom and dad' who give the message, "We are wonderful and good, so you will never do what would hurt us, which means you will be like us, be like what we wanted you to be or like what we see you as - but not like you." The control and enmeshment is enforced as caring.

- Role playing in low functioning families: to keep the family functioning the children are enmeshed into playing roles, taking on adult jobs, responsibilities and acting out. The need for parenting, pride, protection, mediation, and tension relief all bring in a role player to meet the need. The child is enmeshed in the role and the job while experiencing a lack of choice, individuality and loss of childhood.

- Abuse: abuse sets up hypervigilance, awareness of external moods and threats - the recipient is wrapped into the patterns of the abuser and their boundary strength is disintegrated. The abuser holds control and power, the victim is left powerless and bonded. The abuser projects unwanted emotional reality onto the victim.

- Seduction: seduction, covert or overt, results in the engulfing of the child into the affectional and sexual needs of the adult. The child becomes a vessel for the emotional load of the adult. Pat Conroy in the *Prince of Tides* said, "There is no more powerful seduction than the parent's seduction of their own child."

- Scripting and projection: these form a cast where the child is molded to conform with the vision of the parent, not the reality of the child. Parental issues and images are projected onto the screen and the life of the child plays out the film of the parent's whims and fantasies.

- Becoming an extension of a parent: children are set up to live out the parent's dreams and hopes, to do what the adult could or did not do or to become like the adult.

- Rules, myths, and premises: the system may be rigid and the myths and rules powerful enough to engulf the child into terrors, rages, or passivity. Cult families enmesh the vulnerable members in boundariless anxiety ridden lifestyles long after they have escaped the cult. Premises and myths may also control the vision, direction, and destiny of the individual.

- Family loyalties and the need to belong: to belong to this family, to be loyal you must be what the family needs or expects you to be. The paths are unchosen and reinforced by the need to belong. The fears of being ostracized set up the loss of uniqueness. The family members must reflect the family's distorted image of itself.

- Narcissistic parenting: the adult can only love what is a reflection of the parent. The child learns to find parental love by subjugating their uniqueness and becoming the clone or mirror of the parent.

- Defiance: enmeshed in rebellious postures or the need to be different. Surviving by defying the surrounding control or craziness but still controlled and over involved in what is defied. The need to be different supersedes the ability to be oneself. The more controlling the authority the more defiance becomes a viable response.

- Denial: the secrets acted out. The covert sets up compulsion. (See Principle Four). We are driven by the hidden toward the reality of the covert system and the loss of self.

Enmeshment is the most common place to become stuck in life. Most repetitive self destructive behavior and pathology is the offspring of enmeshment. Family members are often left with a repetition compulsion to reenact or react to the problems, denials, addictions, depression, fears, hopelessness, and breakdown of the family they believed they left.

Not long ago during a workshop in Aspen, Colorado a participant who had been sitting with a distressed look throughout the morning session finally spoke up. He said, "I am sick of this stuff on family, I've done my family work, I dealt with my relationship with my father, I've forgiven him and we get along fine now. The problem is, it hasn't done me any good. In my recovery I don't feel like I'm getting there and I don't believe I ever will get there - wherever that is."

I replied, "It seems you're feeling hopeless and like a failure in your recovery." He agreed and I asked, "Are you feeling this way in other areas of your life?" He responded affirmatively, and I again asked, "What is your father like?" He replied, "You're not listening, I dealt with my father." Once more, I asked "Well, what was he like anyway?" He looked at me with a little gleam in his eye and said, "Are you asking me if my father felt hopeless and like a failure?" I said, "Yes." He continued, "My father was not a failure but he always seemed to feel as if he were, he always seemed to believe he was supposed to do something or get somewhere in his life he was never going to achieve." I responded, "Maybe your problem is not in your relationship with your father but in your father's relationship with his own life and the world. You may be enmeshed in a posture and attitude toward life that belongs not to you but to your father." His next comment was how the feeling of hopelessness and failure had been a traveling companion for years, effecting his relationships, career, and recovery. The hope was he would be able to place it where it belonged, in his father's reality or at least he would be able to 'have it' so it would not 'have him.' He had an opportunity to not be dragged down or bound by the heaviness of failures, though he may notice it reentering his reality on occasion, even times when he was succeeding.

CHAPTER 12

ELEVENTH PRINCIPLE
Families Are Governed By Myths, Premises
And Organizing Principles

*Wisdom is listening to past pathmakers who found their way and
left directions for us to follow in story, legend, myth, & song.*
                                                    Reflections

MYTHS

Myth is the belief system of the family enhancing and guiding
the spirit and represents the intangible internal forces and powers.
Myth is found in the tales and images of personal, cultural and family history, supported by customs and rituals. Fast track families
tend to become disdainful of the rituals and dismiss the history thus
losing the powers of myth.

Emptiness, despair and chaos of family, as well as culture, can
come from the absence of myth and its companions, the rituals supporting the myths and dreams growing from it. The symbolic and
mythical meanings of marriage, children, community and spirituality when eroded find inadequate replacements. Sometimes in families, violence, control and aggression replace ritual. Addiction re-
places meaning, wealth and the fantasies of wealth become the
symbols and stuff of dreams and the attempts to overcome shame
and insecurity. Sexual energy and seduction may be substitutions
for family love. Rituals of service become lost in narcissistic

selfishness and doing one's own thing. In many families children are property or extensions of the parents, rather than a miracle of the gift of life itself. When marriage and family have no symbolic meaning, with the true substance of each lost to the stresses and confusion of contemporary lifestyles, each member ends up isolated and wandering.

Holding onto mythology, though difficult, can be done in sharing the stories, reading literature, looking at family history and exploring the rituals. Sometimes the rituals from other families or other cultures and groups can be incorporated to provide more meaning. From the stories in myth and symbol, dreams rise and meaning is enveloped. These dreams, this meaning of what it is to be in this family, of what has been taught about times past, guide through the tough times, present and future. They guide through changes, losses and traumas. While riding on the vehicle of belief, ritual and symbol one can move down the path of self becoming.

The myths of the family may be real or not real, but in the myth is a theme, a story about living supporting a way of behaving and guiding the inner conversations with ourselves, our thoughts. Myths and dreams are founded in the stories told and events related. They may limit noticing, or enhance it, prevent certain events or facilitate them. Myths are the stuff of going beyond, of discovering possibilities in spite of our limitations.

Myths may also be used to control or to prevent noticing what is needed. The myth of stubbornness might prevent the noticing of the need to become stubborn about taking care of or standing up for oneself. The myth may be used to support a role that doesn't work. The myth of independence, mythologies of charm, power, cleverness or freedom may be the cover for selfishness, seduction, scheming, or addiction. The myth may prevent noticing pathology, the myth of a parent's charm may cover sexual compulsion, the myth of the power and authority of a parent may be abusiveness and aggressiveness.

Sally's family held many myths. The myths supported the denial. The mythology of her uncle held him up as a charmer everybody loved, except in fact, her uncle was a sex addict and he seduced nearly every woman he met. The myth of grandma was she was very strong and authoritarian, and held the family together. The reality was grandma was a rageful, abusive controller. The myth of mom was she was a saint, when in fact mom was a very classic enabler, excusing and taking care of Sally's father's alcoholism. In her relationships Sally had a difficult time sorting out strength from abuse, charm from seduction, and enabling from caring.

PREMISES

Premises are the core beliefs of how the family operates. Premises of a family may include beliefs about creation and higher power, a belief in God as a kind and gentle force and a trust in the process of creation. Premises may be constructive or destructive. A more destructive premise may be, "evil is punished and mistakes are evil." There are premises about men and women. Beliefs about gender may support sexism, or reinforce unrealistic expectations or destructive fantasy fulfillment. "Men are no good, they'll only use you and leave you." Some premises support addiction, "feelings must be medicated," "sex is the most important need," or "food is love." Premises are also the basis of our schemas of life and the foundation of spirituality. "The world is benevolent," "people are good and gentle," "given a chance people can be giving and comforting and protecting," "we can find safe places, safe harbors to be ourselves and share our dreams," and "we can realize our fantasies and dreams with the support of others."

The health of a family is reflected in the health of its premises about life, creation, and higher power. Relationships can be a reflection of premise. The premises become a lens of how the world is viewed. The lens is a doorway, we step out into the image of our premises, we make them real. Healthy reality rests on healthy premises.

Jake grew up in the shadow of his brother who was a star student and athlete. Jake's parent's poured lavish attention on his brother and virtually ignored Jake. Jake developed a premise. The premise was, "I must be successful to be noticed." His life began to revolve around his drivenness in work and for success. The more he focused on trying to be successful the more isolated he became. He drove people away with his drivenness. In therapy he finally realized he was only truly successful when he was truly himself.

ORGANIZING PRINCIPLES

Organizing principles are the parameters and operating system effecting individual choices. They are like crests and banners telling of the essence of the system. Principles are generally less specific

110

than premises, they may be based on premises but provide the context and limits of how we operate. Decision and choices are guided by these principles. The principles create multigenerational themes, endeavors, careers, and focus of life energy. Principles are deeper than roles and scripts, more encompassing than rules or premises. Supported by mythology they move us in the direction of the system's flow.

The guiding principle of the family may be pro-social humanitarianism. The emphasis and energy are placed on improving humankind, relieving the suffering of others. Missionary work, social work, philanthropy, advocacy, fund raising, volunteer work are all spun around the guiding principle. Family members react to these principles even when rebelling against them.

The principle may be the arts; creating and preserving beauty in music or other fine arts - specific or generalized. Creating, collecting, commissioning, writing, teaching and studying the arts. Living for beauty flows from this guide. Families of artists and curators, families of musicians and composers listen to the intergenerational voice beckoning them toward the center of family energy.

The principle may be teaching, selling, politics and power, accumulation and control. The call may be sex, seduction, crime and dishonesty, rebellion and sabotage or intelligence. Or the system call may attract one toward adventure, exploration, sport, racing, entertainment, inventing, gardening, environmental protection, books, religion, or science and research.

Not all members of a family follow the principles in career or avocation but all are affected by it and must resist or follow. The principles may be recurrent themes grabbing members periodically or a magnet drawing in most of the family members and energy.

The principle may rest on biogenetic talent, modeled behaviors, expectations and opportunity. It may go beyond these and become part of a family pattern reflected in the myths and premises of family.

In recent American history the Kennedy's appear to be an example of a family with multiple guiding principles seen in the members. These include humanitarianism and philanthropy, political power, accumulation, sex and seduction, and social welfare. Having children is a guiding principle of some families. Bringing children into the world and investing in them may be the purpose of family. Consumption can be seen in other families as the prime objective with accumulation or greed a common principle. Preserving history is a common theme just as 'building' or 'the sea' may be.

We need to be aware of the forces and themes offering direction and meaning. Explore what the lifestyle and interests of family members reflect about the family. Organizing principles are more easily integrated or rejected when understood. Recognizing the principles of family offers choice. Choice is freedom.

CHAPTER 13

TWELFTH PRINCIPLE
The Family System Is Intergenerational

The future of the world does not lie in the hands of children,
it lies in the hands that hold the hands of children.
We cannot hold the hands of children until we hold the hand and
heal the heart of our own childness.

Reflections

The rules, premises, myths, beliefs, roles, styles, choices and many of the behaviors, both destructive and enhancing, appear in families for several generations. Change occurs yet much of the system is maintained. The obsessions or the aberrations that seem like a break in the system and its beliefs are commonly a part of the intergenerational functioning of the family. Studies reflect many families have intergenerational incidents of alcoholism, suicide, depression, mental illness, learning disabilities, incest, or child abuse. Therapists have learned to review family history in clients exhibiting these issues and may be more suspicious at their absence than their presence in prior generations. Some of these can be attributed to biogenetic propensities and much to modeled behavior. Several other aspects of family systems contribute to the repetition including the rules, myths and premises as well as the roles, style of bonding, boundary and enmeshment issues.

Since nothing changes until it becomes real, denial is what fuels the intergenerationality of family pathology. *What we don't pass backward, we pass forward.* With a 'national parent protection' racket in operation, most of us pass on to our children while not passing it back to the source. Even with attempts to contain or eliminate the problems they tend to slip through. Issues in one generation may skip the next but resurface in the third. One who has been neglected in their family of origin may have children and over focus on the children and the family becomes overly child centered. The children may become rather narcissistic, so when those children have children, they tend to neglect them starting the cycle over again. Those of us who have experienced physical violence may react by not teaching or modeling any limits, thus our children do not learn limits or self discipline. When they have children, their lack of impulse control may bring them to being abusive or violent toward their children. Those raised in alcoholic families may have reacted so vehemently against alcohol they become rigid about it. Their children, in defiance, may use or abuse alcohol and with the biogenetic propensity become alcoholic. Shame is an intergenerational issue. When parents feel badly about themselves they tend to project it out in a blame/rage and withdrawal spiral causing the child to feel badly and internalize the shame and do the same in their parenting.

Pathology is generally a reaction to or a reenactment of unresolved childhood issues reverberating through a family system for several generations. The intimacy styles, issues of emotional fluency and emotional repression, ways of surviving and coping, medicating pain through addictions all follow one generation to another. The same issue may appear in a different form. More children of alcoholics seem to suffer from disordered eating than alcoholism. The message in alcoholic families is, "medicate the pain." The modeled behavior may set up a revulsion for alcohol use. Aggression and violence in families can set up passive aggressiveness and withdrawal in subsequent generations. When parents are over achieving the children often do the same but many follow a pattern of under achievement and failure. We react to or reenact the pathology.

Healthy postures, attitudes, interests, beliefs also become intergenerational. Intimacy, interests in music, literature and art, environmental concerns, healthy self care, interest in athletics and exercise can be a part of the ongoing legacy of a family system. The low functioning aspects of families do not cancel out the healthy aspects. Not every member reacts in any predictable way but the intergenerational issues do impact. Sexual shame and repression may set up addiction and obsession in one part of the family, sexual dysfunction or disorder of desire in another, rage and jealousy somewhere else. The only valid generality is sexual issues will result.

In finding one's own path it is important to *avoid* deciding to '*not be like*' the family but rather to decide to '*be like who we are.*' A person becomes controlled by what is defied. To be free involves embracing the ways we are like our families. New choices can only be made fitting for us in the context of setting and background. One can be realistic about change and able to face the things disliked in parents. Change is frequently elusive when forced but while affirming what and who we are and accepting it's okay to be there, change comes more easily. With this is the possibility change isn't needed, the acceptance may be enough.

Positive change and healing are also intergenerational. The hurt and pathology passed on to children cannot be erased but balanced living, self care and intimacy can be modeled and offered.

Positive changes effect those around and those following . Not by giving them a healthy lifestyle, but offering the modeling, to encourage the choice of healthy lifestyle. The ability to choose is freedom, and freedom in families is also intergenerational.

FAMILY MATTERS
The Principles & Roles of Family

SECTION II
FAMILY ROLES

CHAPTER 14
Role Theory

"If All The World's A Stage, I Want Better Lighting"

Broken Toys Broken Dreams

As social beings we do not function well in isolation. Humans operate best within systems, interdependently connected with each other, interacting in ways effecting the system, ourselves and others. In the structuring of societies and the creation of living styles, there is a process of learning how to function in context. To learn one's place, how to contribute and how to survive and thrive.

The vehicle of these operating procedures are the roles. Some are chosen, others assigned, some are opportunities, others burdens.

Much of what we believe and define about ourselves is based on these roles. The roles may or may not reflect true identity, interests and character, but with so much life energy invested in playing these parts, it becomes a struggle to imagine the limitless possibilities and the multiplicity of paths lying outside of and beyond past roles.

The concept of roles and role playing in systems is one of the most intriguing in human behavior and development. Within a discussion of role theory are the issues of operant conditioning, the style of behavior derived through repetitive reinforcements. Roles and lifestyle are often derived from the image and needs of the system. From role discussion the issue of free will arises. Can one make choices for a true spiritual journey and emerging life direction when there is severe scripting and enmeshment into patterns of operating that are essentially role playing rather than personal becoming?

Assigned roles may overlap and smother personality and moral development. The playing of roles in life is not bad or good, evil or holy. Roles are simply a reality. Certain roles become healthy chosen life enhancers, others the vehicles of how one becomes lost and without direction.

The dictionary defines a role as, "a conspicuous part or function performed by anyone." Many pattern forming activities are based on role. Functioning in areas of work, social, spiritual, recreational, or sexual may occur in the context of role performance.

The dictionary definition continues with, "a character in a play." Many have indeed been assigned a script, a part to play by the directors of their lives and the play becomes reality. The scripts are frequently assigned in childhood and worn or reacted to throughout life. The script assignment may be a desirable lead or a bit part with a barely seen entrance. The particular part played is less important than the awareness of it being just a part, and not necessarily related to or reflecting true identity. The part may be related more to the needs of the directors, playwrights and audience. The actors may be loved or hated for these parts played having few other choices than to follow the script. Once handed a script the process of typecasting can begin, always expected to be the same character no matter what the play.

This is true for children and adults. People are often measured not by the context of their lives, but rather by roles which may or may not reflect what is intrinsic, the true character. We are all great actors but some of us were handed lousy scripts.

Most of what has been taught about roles is an over simplification. Theorists and educators tend to focus on a 'four child role' family system approach where each child adapts a primary role in the family. The names of the four roles varies with the teacher and theory and the primary role each person adopts is often based on birth order and usually remains until the discovery of the true self. The four roles are frequently described as the hero, lost child, scapegoat and mascot, or adjuster, placater, martyr, and achiever.

The four role theory is only *loosely* reflected in family reality and falls short of outlining the complexities of family systems. Families are the primary source of personal role development but families are dynamic, changing organisms. People within the system have several roles helping the system survive or flourish while providing a sense of belonging to for individual. As the family changes the roles may change. Roles also overlap, are shared, are left behind and found anew. The roles left behind still leave their mark in feelings, beliefs, actions, and thought processes. The family system and the roles played can be life enhancing or destructive as well as a blend of the two.

The oversimplification of role theory can set up a pattern of denial. If one sees one's self in the role of over achiever and hero, and these become the primary issues they deal with in their renewal and self discovery process, they may find they have missed many other roles having a profound impact on relationships and identity.

A role is a repetitive pattern of behaviors designed to maintain the functioning of a system as well as offering members of the system survival, coping and belonging. As change occurs, roles change. Roles depend on who we are, where we are, where we came from and what time we are there. To be Irish in the United States in the nineteenth century involved an entirely different role structure than most of the twentieth century. Adolescence, religious beliefs, race, career and gender all involve greatly changing roles from one place or time to another.

The roles we play may or may not reflect our identity, but when over identification with the role takes place there can be a loss of self awareness, esteem and the creative drive and will that comes from combining self knowledge and freedom. Role playing can restrict freedom by limiting our choices.

The roles played in the past have a residual impact. There remains a tendency to fall back into the role or aspects of the role in relationship, career and other settings. Some roles are never left, whether they be positive or destructive. The mask and costume appears permanent.

HEALTHY ROLES

In a healthy system healthy roles maintain high functioning. Healthy roles are based on the uniqueness of the individual, the basic system needs, settings and choices. Healthy life roles are chosen, they help develop strengths and character and do not interfere with the development and rights of others. In healthy roles one is free to not always be in the role, they are not defined by the role, nor do they define themselves through the role. In healthy roles support and feedback are given for and about role performance. These roles are based on self awareness and do not require giving up identity, needs, or reality.

Certain roles involve struggle and sacrifice. The sacrifice may be a healthy choice but not when it breeds resentment and despair.

Being used is not a healthy role choice. On occasions when demands necessitate sacrifice, the giving does not involve a loss of personhood but comes out of love, need and respect. Children who have had to sacrifice their childhood for the family continue the role of sacrifice in adulthood, resulting in the anger and despair of living a life of giving of self without ever really having the sense of self to give from.

PARENT CHILD ROLES

Adulthood and parenthood comes with role responsibility. The parent role involves modeling healthy behavior, decision making, creative questioning and learning, setting and modeling limits, providing a base of security with the emotional and physical support necessary for the affirmation and guidance of other family members. Parents provide a reference point for going outside the family system and facilitate outside help when the parent cannot meet a child's needs or resolve the immediate issues at hand.

Healthy adult role includes modeling balance in meeting the needs of self with the needs of others. Healthy adult role includes teaching how to handle frustrations and anxieties. The role of parent in families is best performed by one who has had parenting modeled and has received support from others. They see themselves as more than a parent, not having their worth tied up in their skill in parenting or the success of their children. The ability to take time outs, to have others fill in and give them breaks, helps maintain the strength of the role. The same holds true for spousal roles and work roles.

Child roles in healthy systems include learning, experiencing, creating, discovering and play. *Play is the work of children and curiosity is the field for the learning experience.* Responsibility is role achievement rather than a role burden.

Adolescent roles in families are more difficult to define. Adolescence is a role marked by some independence, accompanied with economic dependence. It is a role of participation and decision, value formation and learning. Intimacy and identity are the key developmental issues of adolescence. Since these are the struggles of most adults as well, it would seem many people are still struggling through their adolescence.

Healthy role functioning includes permission and freedom to risk new postures, to try out and try on various roles. Referring back to the parent role, how does one try it on before committing to a life long role? Spending time with children, nieces, nephews, foster kids, Big Sister/Big Brother programs, and waiting until forming a relationship with someone it would be desirable to share the parenting journey are important processes before entering the role.

Decision is important. Many people entered careers, marriages, and started raising a family without ever really making the decision to be there. The decision is a prerequisite for role success. For many of us, leaving the role is difficult if there was never a real decision to be in or true acceptance of the role. It is difficult to leave a place until we have been there. We cannot leave a marriage until we have been in the marriage, until we have accepted we are married and acted as if we were. The decision to truly be there before leaving often lessens the desire to leave.

Low functioning systems set up unhealthy roles, maintaining the weaknesses of the system. Through these roles members find a place in the pathology. Unhealthy roles are not chosen, they prevent unique personality development and are difficult to leave. Feedback about role performance is rare except for criticism and shame.

Families have needs as do all systems. The needs of a family include nurturing, producing, maintaining, sponsoring, spousing, parenting, mediating, leadership, spirituality, fun and play as well as a way for the family to exist with pride in community. In a family with alcoholism or other patterns of illness and/or pathology, few of these needs may be met by the adults mired down in the sickness. When adults fail their responsibilities and do not provide the nurturing, leadership, spousing or parenting a major role reversal occurs in the family where the children take over the roles of adults and the adults begin to function as children. This is a form of enmeshment. Children become entangled in needs and jobs belonging to others.

Low functioning roles occur when a person takes on a need or responsibility not being taken care of by the appropriate person. Children move in and take over the responsibilities or attempt to meet the needs. These role reversals damage developmental process because they frequently involve a forced entry into adulthood.

Children who are forced into the roles and responsibilities of adulthood before they are through the developmental processes of childhood are unable to truly become adults or to be children. They are stuck somewhere in between, in a never-never land of acting grown up but not being grown up, of acting childish while losing childness.

Many roles involve acting out the parts of the system that are hidden or protected. Some involve meeting the needs of the system

125

not currently being met. These roles do not always match the overt system.

In obviously low functioning families more of the children will look good than bad. The children keep the system going and learn coping and survival skills offering the look of success as they operate in other systems such as school or church, community and athletics. In an apparently high functioning family with deep hidden pathology, the children tend to look worse and act out more since one of the functions of children in a family is to make the covert explicit. A work addicted family is likely to have more lower motivated children than an alcoholic family. When the family system is sick to the point of cruelty and lovelessness, the sociopathic postures are often shared by the majority of family members. When the low functioning family lives in low functioning community the behavioral norm for most members is acting out unless a powerful positive influence is present. Often the positive influence is only seen as positive as a comparison.

Gary's family was poor and lived in the tough section of a large city. His father had been out of the picture since before his birth. He had several half brothers and sisters and it seemed like chaos wherever he went; school, playground, streets, and apartment. Gary had an attitude that kept him in trouble, his role playing involved rebellion and crime.

Gary's mother became pregnant with Gary before finishing high school. The idea of having a child seemed to make her special, she would be loved and needed. She could quit school and receive support money and later get a job. It did not really work, she had four more children and received

126

limited support but more and more felt like she had missed out. She was abusive to the children, slapped them and told them they were bad. She also told them she gave up her education and freedom for them. She was the one who would always take care of them.

Gary eventually spent time in prison having joined a gang and been busted for armed robbery. One of Gary's brothers became a highly ranked professional boxer. In prison Gary became involved with a therapy group and began to see the set up for the destructive roles he played. He dealt with the abandonment by his unknown father, he too had fathered two children and abandoned them, and he realized his need to belong was part of his gang involvement. The most difficult piece for him was about his mother who he protected with a vengeance. He really bought the idea of her sacrifice and discipline when the reality was using and physical and emotional abuse. He saw a film clip of his brother after a major fight where his brother told the cameras how he owed his success to his mother, who he loved and who gave him strength. It was then Gary realized his brother had always been a bully who also abused him while his mother did nothing to stop it. His brother also beat his own wife and children. Gary finally accepted the painful reality of a mother who used her children as an attempt to find a place and when that did not work just used and abused them, venting her anger and frustration on them while neglecting their real needs. This was the beginning of a new sensitivity and conscience in Gary's dealings with the world. His protection of the offending mother kept him in offending postures.

CHAPTER 15
Categories Of Roles - Role Out The Barrel

The path of self becoming is an intricate network of possibilities designed not for destination but for wandering.

THE EXTENSION ROLES

There are several categories of role found in family systems. These various types of roles can help us understand the dynamics, variations and complexity of role patterns. In extension roles children become projections of the expectations, dreams and hopes of the adults in the family. The children become what adults want them to be, believe they are or think they are supposed to be. The child role is to fulfill the adult dreams or to become what the adult could not be. The extension role stems from the view of children many adults hold in our culture - children are there to give life meaning, immortality and fulfill dreams. *Our children are not our children. They belong not to us but are miracles of the gift of life itself.* The extension role reflects a bond between the adult and the child where the child is disempowered.

Parents with empty and unfulfilled lives may have children to fill the emptiness, to grow up and do for them what they couldn't do for themselves, to go further than they did or to live a replica of their lives based on their fears, powers, successes or even failures. Sometimes there is a competition clause saying, "You cannot go beyond your parent." You have to do it the way they did it and become like them or to become what they want you to be, but not happier, nor more successful, wealthy or powerful.

Parents with excess control issues, egocentrism and narcissism tend to *use* children to act as their agents in the world, to go out and be a reflection of them to other people. Sometimes a parent sets up a child for a low functioning life by modeling and projecting certain behaviors and postures that prevent fulfillment. An obsessive, compulsive parent may project their worries and fears and compulsive behaviors until a child is phobic, anxious and fearful. They may force the child to become an extension of themselves by projecting their issues on them.

Many parents force their children to become what they want them to be by not tolerating differences, by minimizing the child's uniqueness and constantly reinforcing what the parent wants to see. The abusive, narcissistic, or over controlling parent will kill the spark and destroy the miracle of childness.

Parents may try to find immortality through their children but they limit the child's spiritual growth and development causing the child to lose balance. Occasionally an adult filled with self hate can only be redeemed by the child. The mission of the child is to make up for the parent's life or to prove the self hate of the parent was wrong, the child will provide the love and sustenance. Children can also become failures so parents will not feel badly about their own lives. Some parents set up their kids to fail because any time a child succeeds it illuminates the parent's lack of success or feelings of failure. Parents are often like the little league father where the child is not out in the field to enjoy the game, the father is not screaming at the child to have 'fun.' The child is a reflection of the parent and must perform well and look good for the parent to feel good. The stage mother keeps pushing the child to perform so she can feel, reminisce or believe the talent belongs to her.

The extension roles effect our ability to choose careers. How many great artists have been lost for having been forced onto a different path because of an aggressive and controlling father or mother? How many people's lives have been filled with frustration or remain empty because of traveling a path laid out for them by often well intentioned but frequently misguided parenting?

As an extension of a parent, one can become an addict, offender, failure, caretaker, musician, athlete, politician, or adventurer. The measure for whether the role is a chosen one or an overlay of someone else's vision is quite simple. Does the role or activity reflect our uniqueness and identity and is there joy in the journey? As extensions one feels joyless and lost, experiencing increasing confusion and despair.

Different children in the same family can become extensions of different needs, expectations or hopes of the parent.

There were three sons in a family, one son at an early age became an athlete and repeatedly had his name in the paper for playing many sports. He started at nine years old but by sixteen had dropped out - an adolescent athletic burn out. Not until his twenties did he realize he dropped out of athletics at sixteen because he had not been supported for doing it for himself, he had been doing it for his father. He realized this on an occasion in his mid twenties when he began to get back into being physically active by running. He ran a marathon and upon completion called his father who, after hearing his son had just finished running a 26.2 mile run, replied that he (the father) was the fastest kid in Pocatello, Idaho where he had grown up. The father did not acknowledge what the son had accomplished but used the son's accomplishment to reminisce, relive and revive the father's potential. It isn't that the father was supportive or pushy about athletics, the father simply used all of the son's athletic endeavors as a way to access his own lost or unfulfilled athleticism. The second son had been involved in several businesses, was obsessed with and addicted to work, but was recycling failure. A pattern the father had also lived. This is the son the father had taken into business at the age of seventeen and made a partner, but a disempowered partner with no control or choices. The third son was charming and very wild and adventure oriented. This son acted out all the 'crazy' stories that he had grown up hearing from his father. This was Dad's 'best buddy' who went out from the family to be the adventurer the father saw himself as, but also like the father, a self destructive lifestyle through the adventures and 'craziness.'

One can be set up to live out a parent's dream or need in many areas including religion. People become priests, rabbis, ministers as extensions of the parent's religiosity. One can even marry and have children to fulfill parents' dreams of the extended family. The problem is not in the choice made, it is in the absence of the ability to choose.

To have expectations, hopes and dreams for children is not wrong or unrealistic, but to force them into a mold, a personality, behaviors, careers or lifestyle because of personal need may be the ultimate sin of parenting, to force someone on a path not belonging to them causes a true loss of spirit and spirituality.

GENDER ROLES

Roles are also based on gender. Roles of Men and Women include culturally taught expectations and norms as well as family messages and peculiarities. In a healthy system there is support for choices of lifestyle and career. The more low functioning the system the fewer choices one has and the more rigid the gender roles are likely to become. Families enforce cultural stereotypes of sex role including; women as sex symbols, child bearers with limitations or beauty objects; or men as economic symbols, expendable worriers, providers and success objects. In families a gender role may become a source of shame, denial of pride in their Womaness or Manness, the joy of becoming a man or a woman. Self hate can flow from systems with postures of woman hating or man hating. Gender role rigidity is found in most cultures and restricts ability to forge a path based on unique personality and interests. It also provides a sense of order and place for people within the culture.

Rigidity can set up inadequacy, arrogance, restrict career choices, effect how we play, what and who we play with, how we identify self and can even effect longevity. Gender role rigidity is one of the contributing factors to men dying, five to seven years before their time. The stressors of men's work, responsibility and competitive expectations can cause stress related terminal illness and shortened life spans.

Little girls who want to play ball and climb trees have been called 'tom boys', however the very term 'tom boy' reflects a gender role rigidity. Why can't a little girl who wants to climb trees and play ball be a little girl who wants to climb trees and play ball, instead of having to be a boy? A sensitive boy is often pressured to toughen up or made fun of, maybe producing the opposite effect, increasing the sensitivity. An aggressive girl child is warned she may become a 'bitch' or 'nag.'

There is a tendency to 'gender identify' qualities and attributes not gender related. Sensitivity in men is not a feminine trait nor is competition or aggression in women a masculine trait. Qualities and traits may be acted out differently, depending on the gender, but both are *human*, not gender qualities. Much of what is attributed to gender is really the cultural norm and expectation, not necessarily based on actual gender differences.

ROLES AND PHYSICAL APPEARANCE

Physical appearance can also determine roles. To look like someone in a family may mean becoming like the person or being scripted to act like them. If one looks like 'crazy' uncle Harry, by the time they are nineteen years old they may be hanging out in junk yards like uncle Harry did.

Physical appearance in our culture has an impact on expectations of others and lifestyle possibilities. A large man with rough features would be reinforced to behave in certain ways. Women are frequently set up for roles because of appearance in our culture with family reinforcing stereotypes concerning hair color, height, body shape or size. Actions based on physical appearance depend largely on how the family deals with each member's physical self. Being teased because of a physical attribute can cause a shameful, clowning, rebellious or defiant role. Being attractive can be a set up to act out a parent's image or fantasy. Attractiveness can bring the burden of being used, lessened expectations of intelligence, being seen as a challenge, jealousy issues, ownership issues, having to prove there is something beyond the looks. People who fit the cultural assessment of beauty get hurt as much as people who do not, but in different ways.

Role expectations are based on the external appearance but real beauty has to do with self esteem and self concept. People in roles and settings preventing them from self acceptance would tend to have less attractiveness than people who are allowed, encouraged and affirmed to be themselves. In a study, the most attractive people in a large group were the people who had a healthy relationship with themselves, a positive self image.

Physical appearance can set up roles, but roles can also effect physical appearance. Victim oriented roles may set up a stooped, tucked in, round shouldered, slumped appearance. A person in an earth mother role may become very large as part of the image and possibly the burden they carry. An angry person may have a certain tense body posture and rigidity. Sexual or physical trauma may be reflected in physical appearance, posture, grooming, hygiene, dress, skin reactions and even body shape and size. Many roles effect how we take care of our bodies, our muscle tone and sometimes the development and growth of our bodies.

ENMESHMENT ROLES

Most low functioning roles stem from becoming enmeshed in the needs of the family system or the projections and hopes of other people in the system. Enmeshment frequently involves acting out the denial and secrets or rules, premises and the lack of boundary formation in family. A child raised in a family with intense covert anger may become a raging offender or remain in a victimized trauma ridden role. A child who's family system was basically dishonest may find a role of crime and criminal behavior. In an alcoholic family the alcoholism inebriates the entire family with the roles of each member of the family stemming from the disease. The alcoholism breaks down healthy physical, emotional, sexual, spiritual and spatial patterns. Low functioning behaviors follow. Everyone is enmeshed in the disease. This is also true for families with other denied illnesses, pathologies or addictions. The family revolves around the addiction or illness and each person develops roles as reactions or coping mechanisms for the denied and hidden pathology. More on enmeshment in Section I, Chapter 10.

When adults are not meeting the system's needs the children plug into these unmet needs taking on roles they cannot successfully fill. In this disintegration of family, enmeshment occurs and children lose their boundaries and identity. They lose the sense of uniqueness and preciousness a healthy childhood offers. The developmental path is lost and they become broken toys with broken lives.

BONDED ROLES

The issues around inappropriate bonding form a distinct role grouping. Bonding is a necessary and healthy form of attachment, teaching security and value. Bonding can be pathological when over done or inappropriate as discussed in the section on Family Principles. Bonding must allow space for the emerging development and changes of each individual. Over bonding becomes bondage and can cause rebellion. Over bonding occurs when the needs, pain or helplessness of a parent sets a child up to meet the parent's needs or provide support. A child may be the appointed source of nurturing for the parent.

The power differential between parents may effect the bonding process. Some children attach to or bond with the greater power, identifying more with the dominating parent. Others are selected to care for and bond with the parent who seems to be more powerless. The child will likely become personally more victim oriented when closer to the parent in the victim role. Continued bonding with aggressors is reenacting the offender behavior and victim role. Becoming responsible for a person in the family who is victim-ized can set one up for a life of being used with occasional forays into aggression.

Inappropriate bonded roles are set up by many forms and devices. Over control and abuse can form bondage as well as seduction and manipulation. A child may receive excess atten-tion from one parent, be noticed more, talked to or held reinforcing the bond. The bond is abused when it is used for a surrogate role, a role reversal where the child becomes like a spouse or best buddy to the parent or is repetitively in the position of parenting the parent. This bonding often takes place through a seduction process where the child is courted, even romanticized. The parent may share in-terests and emotional time, use deep self disclosure, teasing or flirtation. This bonding is a form of abuse. Children who are 'used' are abused, it is a velvet glove abuse usually unnoticed and undealt with. The repercussions of these bonds in one's life are enormous. The undealt with, unprocessed emotional bond of a child with a parent can produce a series of relationships where one is used. It can cause a fear of intimacy stemming from the fear of being used by others or acting out by repetitively using others. One may reenact past bonded roles by using children while avoiding intimacy in adult relationships. Bonding with children is positive and a need. It only becomes abusive when it is repetitively done with the child meeting the needs of the adult. Is the adult there when the child needs affection and noticing or the child there when the adult needs affection and noticing?

Sexual or physical abuse can also cause this bonding. Abuse is an enslavement process bonding the victim to the victimizer. One of the primary reasons battered women have a difficult time leaving battering relationships, maybe for decades, is they are enslaved and bonded to the abuser. They are placed in a role involving loss of power, identity, and choices. Over time they become more dependent on the abuser and may even have a difficult time imagining being alone. The same dynamic happens to children being battered, abused or severely neglected. The bonded role deepens as the neglect or abuse escalates. The child loses the sense of personal power and their survival depends on the moods and whims of the parent. They play a part within the violence but do not choose or direct their script or actions.

Bonded roles also occur in systems with frequent enabling. In addicted families or families with a controlling, sick or mentally ill parent the enabling bond is frequent. There is a collusive or conspirative partnership between either the addicted parent or the spouse and the child. Both parents telling children secrets can break down the healthy boundary between the parent and the children causing enmeshment and over bonding.

Parents who need affection, feel lonely and isolated will often turn to a child to meet these needs. The child may experience this as affection, even though they are being used. A child survives by imagining the mythical bond, a fantasy of the parent being loving and available, and they will survive and thrive because the parent cares for them. The reality known internally or on a subconscious level is they must be available to the parent and are being used. Because of this using relationship the child becomes more and more defended internally. This inner shield is partly based on fear for survival. The fantasy bond is a survival technique for the protection of self. The parent who has over bonded to the child is commonly placed on a 'pedestal' by the child, remaining there even after the parent has abandoned or hurt the child in other ways. A child internalizes the abandonment and hurt and experiences it as being something wrong with them, the child. Subsequent self blame and being used causes the child to become more and more defended, often unable to sustain healthy relationship at any point in their lives. The child frequently maintains the myth of the parent's love through adulthood, keeping the parent on the pedestal, holding on to the fantasy bond. Other relationships cannot live up to this fantasy - often they seek the fantasy in partners, but the partner fails. The reality of the using, obsessive relationship with the parent becomes reenacted in a series of failed, using relationships with partners.

Commonly in the parent/child inappropriate bond is a sexual energy and seduction process. This can overwhelm or frighten the child so they attempt to detach from the sexual energy of the relationship with the parent. This detachment frequently causes a pattern of disconnection between intimacy and sexuality. Casual sex, non intimate sex is possible, but maintaining intimacy and sex together over time is virtually impossible. Subsequent intimate relationships may be marked by sexual withdrawal and acting out. Being sexualized by the energy in the bonding and enmeshment process with the parent can also set up sexual compulsion, romanticized and sexual fantasies preventing real intimacy or possibly a repulsion, a fear of smothering and images that dissipate or overwhelm sexual energy. Sexual compulsion is on one end of the continuum, while 'sexual anorexia' is on the other. The inability to be sexual is the 180 degrees flip side from obsessing and compulsive behavior. In the 'sexual anorexia' extreme, the parental seduction has fallen on fallow ground, the shutting down makes one immune to the process, memory or recollection as well as the reenactment of the emotional or sexual incest dynamic as portrayed in the over bonding.

This form of emotional incest can produce many of the characteristics of physically acted out incest. The bond can be a same sex or other sex bond. In the same sex bonded role the child may be the best buddy to the parent, a friend the parent never had or the parent's confidant, though it may appear as though the parent is the confidant to the child. When it seems as though one parent is the confidant and the other absent or abusive, a closer look is needed to see if perhaps the child is really the parent's confidant. Again, was the parent there for the child or the child there for the parent?

Parents can bond with more than one child and one child can be bonded to both parents. A similar type of bond can take place with grandparents, uncles and aunts. Often children are sent to live or stay with close relatives and even though the child may enjoy the time spent with that relative, it may even be the best times of childhood, the question remains, is the child there to take care of the relatives' or grandparents' needs? Are they being used? Or were they there because it was a good place for the child? And was the relative there to take care of the child's needs? If it is the child taking care of the relatives' needs a pattern may appear of the child not being able to notice when they are being used, often getting into situations through adulthood where they give and keep giving and eventually burn out because they are not receiving enough in return to keep replenished.

When the child becomes a surrogate spouse or best buddy to a parent, everyone in the family is effected. The siblings may feel jealous and left out. The dynamics are unbalanced. It effects the bonded child because they are being abused in a way that does not feel like abuse and they are often rejected and hurt by siblings or the other parent. Sometimes, however, they are protected from the other parent because that parent doesn't dare abuse the prince or princess. It sets up a triangulation. If the other children are being abused differently, more overtly, or neglected more, the special bonded child feels guilty and may even set themselves up for punishment later in life out of the guilt. The bonded child also ends up feeling lost because they can never reenact the special parental relationship with future partners except in relationships of using or being used.

Millie was married to a violent alcoholic for sixty years. She had been battered, injured in accidents, watched her children be beaten, and the object of great rage. When the rage settled down or her husband sobered up he was remorseful and often bought her elaborate gifts to assuage his guilt. Millie knew she should leave but could never stay away for more than one night.

She attended an ALANON group and someone suggested therapy. In her first therapy session she spoke of her father who abused her brothers, sisters and mother but never laid a hand on her - at least in anger. Her father favored Millie and bought her presents on a regular basis. Millie felt deep guilt and shame about the family abuse and being singled out by not being abused. She also loved the attention and gifts. It made sense for her to be bonded in a relationship where she too was the object of violence but also continued to receive the presents. After one session Millie went home, packed her bags and left. Her written message to her husband was to call her when he completed treatment for his alcoholism.

He did and they are building something new.

The bonded parent may abandon the child after using them, especially with father/daughter bonding. In mother/son bonding usually the son is set up to feel he has abandoned the mother. Once the father has abandoned the daughter, the daughter feels responsible for the abandonment. She feels there is something wrong with her, and because of this feeling of being flawed, she has a tendency to be used and abandoned in future relationships. For more on boundaries and bonding, see *Broken Toys Broken Dreams,* Chapter Eight, BRAT Publishing.

TYPE CASTING AND SCRIPTING

A child may enter a phase of behavior or develop an interest and with the pressure and reinforcement of other family members never be able to break free of the phase, becoming typecast to remain in the posture. Scripting pressures one to become what others see, a projection of what they want or need. Shyness may become the expectation, efforts to come out and be noticed are treated negatively or teased away. This type of reinforcement can set one up to become the charming one, pessimist, the slow one, the ugly one, the sneaky one, the spiritual leader, the artful dodger, or perhaps even the lady killer for Mom or seductress for Dad. The type casting places one in various roles very difficult to retire from. Identity becomes encased in the role. The role is left only by abandoning one's place in family and risking the loss of the social group as arranged by others. To venture out in discovery and try out new ways of operating becomes a risk wrought with tension. The transition between abandoning the group and embarking on a personal journey is a frightening one. It is very difficult to give up a sense of belonging and identity. Allowing the unfolding of self requires courage and support.

The day in and day out methods of survival and acceptance winning one works out as a child to fit family rituals also become roles. Because the roles are crucial to belonging in family the role is confused with identity and survival. An unconscious transference to the role can take place. One begins to believe they are the role whether it be victim, addict, defender or hero. The over identification involves an inability to see other possibilities. Add to this the tendency toward over simplification, the belief each person has one of the four commonly taught roles and the possibility of doing the unraveling is eliminated. To see only the mascot or hero role may cause one to miss being an extension of parent, bonded to a parent, being the mediator, caretaker, addict, victim, collusive, little parent or spiritual leader. Often the role one is willing to embrace such as hero or caretaker is misleading and false. These roles often support delusion and grandiosity and mask the truth.

Scripted roles are similar to type casting and are based primarily on what the child is led to believe about who and what they are. Overt and covert enforcement for choices and directions are the scripting processes. The child is hypnotized and brainwashed into the images and fantasies held by others. Among other things the scripting may be a typecast based on gender, physical appearance or scripts from fairy tales or mythology. These roles may stem from the whims and dreams of parents, the need for fulfillment of their lives. They may be the reenactment of myth, truth or lies from past generations. When influential people tell how one will end up, often one heads in that direction whether if fits or not. Children are frequently scripted by the dreams and fears instilled and projected by others. Some families of musicians, doctors, artists or masons are required to maintain their tradition. Because of genetic abilities and modeling much of it would occur naturally, but force versus choice damages the ability to integrate and maintain the success and sense of pride and comfort with life's choices. The traditions of the family can become a script for life.

Even fairy tales can script. A familiar story read or told can spark an imagined path and compulsive need to live out the story. One can wait forever for the knight in shining armor to come dashing by on the white horse to take us away into the sunset. (Usually to live with his mother!) We can sleep our lives away waiting for Prince Charming and the kiss that brings us to life. We can work and toil while waiting for the pumpkin carriage to arrive, taking us away to find the prince. One can kiss toads and frogs until they are blue in the face, even marry one, waiting for the toad to become a prince. We can become Peter Pan and never grow up. We can be heroes, searching for the golden fleece, slaying dragons. We can become Prince Charming, seducing all the princesses we pass by. In the absence of belonging and identity and in the stifling of the dreams rising out of self awareness, one is vulnerable to the images of childhood tales and stories. The fantasies of legend giving rise to courage and meaning when grounded in guardianship and nurturing may give rise to a windmill chasing life of failure and futility when grounded in loneliness and hurt.

Within the favorite stories of childhood are common themes offering life direction. These themes can teach what is needed, what is valued and what must be left behind. Story telling reflects guiding themes which roles support. Writing one's story or telling it, real or imagined can illustrate the patterns and repetitions spiraling us toward present settings. Telling the stories teaches while allowing alterations to the script and inviting new parts to be played. New parts, characters and symbols can enhance rather than stifle adventure.

Significant events of the past can predict future roles. Early abandonment can lead to a role of repetitively being abandoned or lost. An early heroic act can set up the seeking of the attention through fabricated heroics and misadventures. How others react to a period of one's life or incidents can cause a movement toward reenactment that builds roles. An early trait such as curiosity may be the parent's cue to over focus and push the child toward a career based on that trait. Early success with building blocks or Legos™ may trigger the parent obsession to have the child become an architect when in fact it was the parent's dream to become the architect. The roles learned in family can become life scripts. A caretaker in a family moves into care taking jobs for the aged, or entering the nursing profession or ministry. The mediator of the family may find work in labor relations negotiations. The family counselor becomes a licensed family therapist. The same roles are maintained while moving from amateur status to paid professional.

ROLES AND ADDICTION

Within a role exists a complex system of habits, feelings and thought processes functioning similar to an addiction. (*Addiction is a repetitive, pathological relationship with a mood altering substance, event, experience or activity causing major life problems.*) The role may support addiction and may have addictive qualities. Low functioning family roles require the repression and denial of feelings. In the performance of the role there is a mood altering quality reinforcing a repetitive need for self medication.

Even after successfully altering past roles, times of stress, anger or poor self care can facilitate a slide back into these roles. Addictive processes do the same. Workaholism is a role based addiction. Frequently the workaholic is a child who developed a productive role, was reinforced for working hard, and being goal oriented. The role eventually becomes work addiction. The nurturing caretaker in the family becomes compulsive about taking care of others as an avoidance of their emptiness or pain. The family hero develops an insatiable and compulsive need for being noticed, for success, or for the intensity coming with heroics. Carl Eller, the former NFL star speaks of 'heroism addiction' and the 'crash' he experienced when he stopped playing football. The charmer or a seductive role may lead to an addiction to seduction. The compulsive behaviors themselves set up the 'addict' role with the identifying characteristics of control, impatience, mood swings, denial and distortion of reality. Control and power are addictive processes and many of the roles of family are built on the need to control or act out power trips. The family genius may constantly intellectualize to avoid emotional reality. The raging offender becomes addicted to the intensity and the cathartic release of the projected rage, a 'rage-aholic.' The rage is compulsively used as a denial of other feelings and a cover-up, becoming a recurrent and unchosen behavior pattern causing harmful consequences. The rage itself can push one toward the role of offender or into crime which are also addictive processes.

The symptom bearer or scapegoat of the family who carries the family pathology may compulsively act out criminal behaviors. The crime becomes an addiction. Crime addiction is a common addiction but has gone unnoticed and untreated as an addiction. The criminal is in a role and playing out a part just as the hero is, just as the caretaker is. They are driven by the same insatiable compulsions as the alcoholic or gambler.

The role of risk taker or rebel can lead one into intensity addiction. Intensity is the quickest and most effective way to alter brain chemistry, change feelings and shroud pain.

Within the addict role is the ability to switch addictions but still maintain the role. In the alcoholism field, this is called 'dry drunk' syndrome. While not acting out a particular addiction one is still acting out the role of addict. Usually the person in the addict role is also in an enabling role. Addicts tend to enable other addicts, sometimes people with the same addictions, sometimes different. Enablers have a style of living and behaving which supports addiction. This enabling is learned early in families by the no talk rules, learning to not make waves, to not notice, need, or confront. Denial and repression of feelings, hyper-vigilance and over responding to the needs of others is initiation into enabling and addiction.

EMOTIONAL ROLES

Feelings also effect roles. Some roles are based on shame. In the shame based role one's true identity is hidden. Disappearing, manipulation, defensiveness and self destruction are common themes. Addiction roles are frequently based on denied and repressed feelings. Internalized fear can set up the role of an overly cautious 'wall flower', or perhaps the opposite reactions may prevail with excessive risk and 'dare devil' behavior used as a way of giving the fear focus and expression. Pain and suffering may bring about a 'sad sap' depressed role, a victim posture. Excess guilt promotes care taking and codependent roles. The need to fit in becomes a 'chameleon' posture, always being what others need, the ability to blend in with surroundings. Anger can set up the role of bully or offender. Turned inward anger can cause depression and self abuse, a role of self-beration.

Most roles involve enmeshment in someone else's ideas, dreams, behaviors, postures, feelings, and attitudes. Enmeshment also stems from violence. An entire family reverberates to violent incidents. The reverberations include role formation around the violence. Roles stem from overt or covert abuse, neglect or abandonment. Primary roles stemming from violence are the victim, offender and collusive or enabling role. Members of violent families are not restricted to one particular posture, one can move in and out of these roles or operate simultaneously in all three.

CHAPTER 16
Specific Family Roles - What's My Line

To be able to chose a role and play it well is an act not a malady.

The following is a list of specialized roles played out by family members for a variety of reasons. A member may have one or more of the following.

Symptom Bearer

Low functioning systems with denial require a symptom bearer, someone to act out the illness, to reflect it in their lifestyle or identity. This is the 'identified' patient, seen also as the 'sick' or 'crazy' one, or underachiever. They may also become an addict or an offender. Family pathology is inevitably acted out, there are no secrets in families, only denial. Acting out the illness becomes the role for the symptom bearer. The symptom bearer may also eventually help the family by exposing the deeper pathology and become the vehicle for moving the family into a helping resource. The adolescent who is constantly in trouble, the child who develops emotional disturbances, the member with mental illness is often the way the entire family gets counseling. Once the entire system is observed it can possibly be redefined and redirected.

Many families keep a facade of normality and functionality. Pathology is seldom overtly expressed except through children. The child as symptom bearer wears the family pain and pathology. The symptoms may be physical problems, acting out, emotional or mental disorders, addiction or crime. The family seems to revolve around the child but the child is revolving around the family. The problem acts as a distraction from the real issues, usually hidden adult pathology or addiction, marital problems or even mental illness in one or both parents. A symptom bearer may internalize the belief of badness suggested by their symptoms. They are actually more congruent in their responses to the sickness in the family than other family members. If the symptom bearer gets better and leaves, someone else in the family usually gets worse and moves into the role.

It is through the noticing of the symptom bearer that much of family systems theory owes its origins. Founders of family systems theory working with clients who had improved over time and were sent back into their family system, noticed when the client returned for routine follow-up, they were as sick as when they first entered the clinic. When a client had gone through the clinic and did not return sick, the therapists discovered someone else in the family became sick. The symptom bearer is often a service provider for in the process of dealing with the symptoms of a member the family may be involved to the extent the real issues come out and change begins. Symptom bearers usually feel flawed, different, separate and anxious. They have a tendency to bear the symptoms and react to hidden pathology of what ever system they operate in. They are often blamed for the despair or other family problems and have difficulty finding or accepting support. Other names for the role include identified patient, the sick one, crazy/odd one, or the family problem. The symptom bearer is frequently also the scapegoat.

Scapegoat

The scapegoat has been violated by patterns of repetitive blame, abuse or shame. The victimization may be obvious or subtle. It differs from the victimization of other family members, not necessarily in type but in the control, blame or repetition. The scapegoat is seen as the cause of family tension and problems, and often acts out in ways justifying this view. Scapegoating can begin at anytime from birth to adulthood and can last a short period or a life time. Long term scapegoating is more frequent than episodic or short term. Physical or verbal attacks are the usual expression of the blame and hostility towards the scapegoated child. Demeaning names and repeated attacks on performance, ideas or behavior erodes self image and confidence.

The scapegoat internalizes the blame from the system into repressed shame. Shame controls subsequent behavior and relationships thereby reinforcing itself. The unresolved anger and rage in the parents' lives and relationships is projected at the scapegoat and pressed into the fabric of their identity until it unravels in random, angry and defiant behaviors. Out of the repressed hate and shame comes a pattern of self and other destructive activities, which become the family rationale for the original scapegoating.

The scapegoat may counter the shame by arrogance and over confidence. Low functioning systems need the scapegoat to maintain denial. The family is a microcosm of a puritan culture with the belief that we are good, pure, holy and right. Evil and problems must come from the outside. Cultures blame minorities or outside influences; African Americans, Jews, Catholics, drug dealers, Communists.

Families find one member to focus on as well as the outside influences. The problem is the child but the family is okay.

In low functioning families, the pain, anger and shame in the parents and between the parents may eventually destroy the system unless directed elsewhere. To project it on a child releases the pressure allowing the family to remain intact. In some respects, the scapegoat holds the family together but also by acting out becomes the town crier, telling the community of the family pathology. Not all scapegoats do serious acting out. Some act in, with more 'self' than 'other' destructive patterns. The scapegoat can be an underachiever or an overachiever, caretaker or rebel, nice or mean. Other roles or qualities interact with the blame system but do not supplant it. Scapegoats use self blame as a survival tool, believing something is wrong with them and if they change, the blame system and abuse they live with will also change. This gives them a sense of empowerment, control and hope rather than the terror of having no power to alter the sick system. The self blame fuels the shame, acting out and blame cycle. If two children in a family do exactly the same behavior, the one in the scapegoat role will be punished more or differently.

The anger in the scapegoat role can be used as a source of resolve to succeed and strength to overcome obstacles. It can also turn into apathy or be acted out in rage. In certain kinds of competition the anger may give the scapegoat an edge. In some settings, such as contact sports, it may give them a family hero role although this will be short lived. Scapegoats tend to revolve around victim-offender and collusive-enabling issues in relationships. Their post trauma effects include mood swings, chronic stress, addictions, intensity seeking and emotional disorders. They seldom realize or understand the impact of the scapegoating in their self destructive lifestyle.

Many develop protective and care taking postures toward vulnerable groups and victims, though they may easily move into the blaming posture they have learned and become hurtful of others. Poor self image, internalized shame, self destructive behaviors can be life themes. The scapegoat can use their defiance and anger as a way of finding success. Unless they deal with their defiance and the hurts of childhood they usually find their success rather limited and eventually go back to being self destructive. Other terms describing the scapegoat role include sacrificial lamb, the bad seed, family victim, black sheep, the bad kid, and problem child. In violent families, the violence is usually encapsulated on one child more than others, even families without overt violence one child is usually blamed more or viewed differently than the others. Most violent offenders were in a scapegoat/victim role in childhood and many are very protective of the parents who hurt them.

Overachiever

Families have a need to be accepted in the community where they live. When parents are low functioning, the children often react to the humiliation and loss of community pride by succeeding, over achieving and looking good. This makes the family look good. *The successful child is not in less pain than children who are failing or acting out.* They may be more adaptive or have simply been selected for a more successful appearing role. The success is shallow and not usually a source of fulfillment to the child. The family expects accomplishment from the overachiever but they seldom experience the good feelings from their success. They are exploited to make the family appear healthier and their success does not fix anything, it just makes things look better.

A low functioning family has a high need to maintain denial of pathology while functioning within community. The children who are successful help maintain the denial and build community pride. As a child succeeds the family takes credit for the success. The successes are shared, failures are blamed. Given how well the child is doing, "the family cannot be that bad," or "the parents must be doing something right." The adults can focus on the achiever as the norm and if the other children do not measure up, there must be something wrong with the other children.

The need to exist and function within community is facilitated by the overachiever. Through the successful child the family establishes a prideful connection with the community. The pathology is painted over by the success of the child. Overachievers may be limited and specific in their success or they may be children who succeed at most of what they do. Their real failure is felt internally since they can never really do enough to make the sick family well. Since the family is *using* the success to cover the pathology, the over achiever seldom feels good about accomplishments while experiencing pressure to accomplish more.

The role may be a life time of high visibility and accomplishment accompanied by internal inadequacy. It may alternate with periods of overt failure. Occasionally a child may find a niche where they excel for a period of time and have a short run as the family hero. Parents will frequently view the accomplishments more as their own than of the child. The child's success accesses parental dreams or history and is separated from the uniqueness of the child. Overachievers often become *human doings* rather than *human beings*. They spend much of their life working at being, looking or doing good rather than having fun or being playful. They may play and do it well but the energy is on appearance and performance not enjoyment. Like the sibling parent, they have grown up too soon. The loss of childhood spells the impossibility of adulthood. The role is wrought with inadequacy, anxiety, and occasionally arrogance. Tension, stress and anger are held within, especially the anger at being ripped off. The rip off may continue by being used by organizations or agencies and even friends.

Other terms for the overachiever include hero, star, perfect child or the responsible one. Acceptance comes through success. The pain level of the successful child is not less, it is just not always as visible.

The Sibling Parent

When parents do not fulfill the duties of parenting, the task falls to the children to parent each other. One child often takes on the majority of parenting functions while others take on jobs intermittently or for specific needs. The primary parent role is usually filled by the first or second child for obvious reasons, but any child can become the little parent. The parenting offered may be gentle and nurturing or cruel and controlling. The job is to keep the family functioning at some level and to deal with daily needs. The parent role may include household functions; cooking, cleaning, laundry, organization for school, enforcing rules around curfew and homework. Little parents may be the ones who arrange health care, teach hygiene, advise and nurture as well as discipline. Organizing in larger families can be an all consuming task.

The little parent is seldom childlike and playful, often seen as bossy, mean, distant and serious. There is little childhood within the role. It is much different than playing house. It is an overwhelming and often depressing burden to have the primary responsibility for another person's child while still a child. This role is a set up for introspection, isolation and an over controlling lifestyle. Adulthood may be a replay of the role, personally and professionally. One may feel imprisoned by their progeny. The little parent also may react against the role with a refusal to have or to work with children, although this is less likely.

The role diminishes the ability to make choices about having children and enjoying the play ground of parenthood and parenting. Childness must be embraced by adults before children can be enjoyed. The little parent's imprisonment can extend into other aspects of life. Loss of spontaneity, controlling or care taking relationships and feeling entrapped by life circumstances.

Many of us parented our siblings, often out of love or concern, frequently out of survival. The parenting carries the responsibility and pain of parenting without the pleasure and privileges. When the child parented by a sibling succeeds the pride of success is for the parents or family, not the sibling parent. When the child parented experiences difficulties or dies the sibling parent is seldom allowed the feelings, the grief that accompanies witnessing one's child in trouble or lost. The sibling parent is more often blamed than praised or thanked. After a time a sibling parent is seen as meddling or over involved rather than appreciated or understood. The controlling posture facilitating survival may become the force driving family members and possible friends further away.

The sibling parent role is marked by anxiety, inadequacy, control and worry. Often there is a greater ability to care for others than self. This role may include the companion roles of lost child, spiritual leader, caretaker and occasionally family hero. Other terms for the sibling parent role include bossy one, little parent, or family general. The sibling parent role may be filled by cousins and even occasionally baby sitters or neighbors get into the act.

The Mediator

Conflict is a part of any system or group. A job of parenting is to provide mediation and conflict resolution. In many families conflict stems from the parent's relationship or their individual pathology and is recycled in the daily lives of other family members. When parents are the cause of the conflict and anger they are unable to help with the resolution. The symptomatic eruptions of sibling and family anger become irritations that enter the wellspring of adult rage. Parental involvement can escalate the conflict. Adults may over react, feel helpless or become passive/aggressive. The conflict becomes a potentially dangerous commodity so again, the child comes to the rescue, a new role is born, one of mediator. The mediator tries to bring peace and prevent escalation. The problem solving child may be in the middle of several conflicts at any given time. Much of their energy goes into counseling and mediating the parent's relationship, if a relationship is still visible. The rest goes to quelling other family disturbances. Eventually the mediator sets up shop in school, community, politics, industry perpetually offering suggestions for peace and fairness, fighting injustice and manipulating power differentials to at least overtly reflect balance.

The mediator is constantly 'mucking' around in other people's concerns whether called on to do so or not. The mediating may be one of the jobs of a sibling-parent role but generally the sibling-parent reacts to conflict the way adult parents do, with enmeshment and hyper-reactiveness. The mediator is frequently relationship oriented. Third kids do great mediation. Mediators have a more difficult time with their own conflicts, often avoiding their personal issues. It is so much easier to focus on others. Mediators tend to become covertly controlling. A deep sense of futility and frustration stems from their inability to mediate the key conflict in the family, the adult relationship. They may become bonded to one parent as an attempt to fill some of the needs and thereby enable the parent to remain in the relationship. Mediators frequently get rejected or scapegoated because of their involvement. Their best career choices involve labor relations negotiations or marriage counseling. Other names for the mediator include placater, meddler, and problem solver.

Lost Child

Enough has been written about the lost child to have found most of them. In the workings of a family with demands and needs for nurturing and attention, there is frequently a feeling and belief there is not enough to go around. This is a reality. There is not enough to go around so certain children go without. They are not noticed, enjoyed or fussed over. One way to get noticed is to act out but some children endure silently. They become the lost children. They are not usually entirely lost, just slightly visible. They generally do well at following the family rules, don't make waves, don't notice, don't question, don't feel, and don't create problems. In some respects most of the children in impaired families are lost and virtually all of their childhood is lost, but there are peculiarities to the lost child role. A sense of isolation and separation from the family pervades the role. Not being noticed or connected sets up further withdrawal. The invisibility crosses over into other settings, especially school and friends. Loneliness and depression are frequently part of being lost. The lost child feels more lost in contrast to the over bonded, abused and scapegoated siblings.

When lost children attach, they tend to over attach driving people away with their dependency needs. The other children in the system can be a source of envy, even the one victimized. Negative attention is at least attention. The child can be in the lost child role for a period of time as a transition before discovering other possibilities. Some lost children feel more like orphans. They do not seem to belong to the family and are not of the family. Their birthdays may be forgotten, appointments not followed up on, left behind on vacation, home alone with sitters, and very few pictures in the photo album.

Lost children, even when grown up have a difficult time feeling a part of things. They feel like outsiders in their nuclear families, social groups and work settings, not included in things, nor noticed for promotions or even their presence remembered in reminiscing. They may also move around a lot, believing in a geographic cure for their lack of connection to a place or people. Lost children have felt their loneliness for so long it becomes like an old friend, safe and secure as well as sad. The role may breed independence but is not a role of independence. The lost child, young or old, may be nearby, and around, yet they are just more difficult to notice. Teachers forget their names, bus drivers forget their stop and the supper table often gets set one place short.

Lost children feel sad and separate but seldom make a fuss. They avoid flamboyance and tend to attach to other lost children. Lost children are set up to attach to offenders who notice and then use. Even when the lost child role is of short duration the impact can remain in adulthood. Other terms for lost child are orphan, missing one, wanderer, or wallflower. Lost children feel unsettled and have a difficult time belonging.

Rebel

The rebel is a reactor, externalizing the defiance towards authority most children of impaired families feel. Rebels learn to survive through rebellion but the rebellion itself becomes a source of their undoing. Much of it becomes self destructive acting out or the refusal to acknowledge valid authority and genuine guidance.

A rebel may be the scapegoat rebelling against the blame, the former hero defying expectations and pressures, the extension of the parent struggling to find a path of their own or simply a strong willed defiant personality refusing to immerse in the family brand of 'craziness' or sameness. The rebel usually operates in the paradigm of the system. The defiance towards authority, internal and external may be part of the family system so the defiance really isn't all that defiant. Acting out and rebellion may be done in ways supporting the system. In an alcoholic family a child may rebel and end up chemically dependent as part of the rebellion. The same can be seen in families with dishonesty or rage. There is a bit of the rebel in most adult children of low functioning families. It is a natural yearning to be on one's own path and to resist all the pressures from external sources pulling and pushing. The rebellion can be channeled in recovery to help react against the pathological, negative impact of the family. This has limited success however because reacting against something usually gives power to it. In the reaction against, we usually go to the opposite extreme and the opposite of sick is still sick, the opposite of something is generally the same, it is even on the same line.

A period of rebellion is common in adolescence. Rebels can be very creative after they learn to embrace or channel their anger. Rebels often are the leaders of reform be it political, consumer activism, civil rights, art or education. They frequently lead us into new expressions in art, literature and architecture, alter our way of viewing reality and may express great courage in promoting change. They see the fallacies and myths and expose them. On the other hand, they are capable of setting up great scams and much of the criminal activity of the culture. Rebels in the extreme become sociopathic and anti community, not respecting even necessary rules and authority. Rebels generally feel anger accompanied by shame and a repression of fear driving them towards fearlessness. They may alter reality to fit and fuel the rebellious process. Another term for rebel is the defiant one.

The Oracle

The oracle is the font of wisdom, direction, guidance and insight. Family members turn to the oracle to understand the past and predict the future. The oracle is frequently set up to give advice and they move easily into the counselor role. The advice is seldom heeded, even when it is good advice. Oracles spend much time figuring out the system so they can feel less 'crazy.' They attempt to rise above their emotional reactions and involvement and use their feelings as sources of insight. They frequently study psychology, or plan to, but less frequently enter the field of psychology. Maybe because there are so few answers to their dilemmas. They tend to philosophize in lieu of psychologize. They notice a good deal and frequently have deep insights into the family. Keeping a little distance helps support the mystique they promote as well as providing less challenge to their need for control and to be right. Oracles frequently use their insight for manipulation and survive through introspection and thinking their way out of problems. They may have relationship problems because of their analytical, anti-emotional or controlling postures and are forever over processing problems. The oracle also goes by the name philosopher, guru, analyzer or family psychologist. They may suffer from introspective depression, especially if a parent was chemically dependent or mentally ill. They own large libraries of partially read books. Sometimes the oracle role is blended into the healer or medicine man role with a sincere focus on resolving, reframing and healing emotional hurts and losses.

Mascot

Tension in low functioning families becomes a dangerous commodity often exploding in anger and violence. The job of the mascot is to ease the tension, to distract and diffuse through humor and cuteness. The mascot may be cute by virtue of being the youngest, or most attractive or funny, or they may entertain through personality and persistence. They may be humorous because of antics, risk, klutziness or mimicry, or they may be clever and amusing by virtue of intellect and a quick wit using play on words and clowning. A playful approach can work wonders in helping family members to refocus conflicts and diffuse pressure.

Mascots generally minimize their own pain, anger and fears. They seldom take themselves seriously and the rest of the family follows suit by not taking them seriously. They act out their family role by clowning around in school, with friends, and often under achieve in spite of high potential or brilliance. They are frequently verbal and social while hiding their loneliness and social anxiety. Picture the sadness behind the clown face. Mascots frequently charm their way out of trouble but may also clown their way into it.

Their playful approach can have an edge of meanness and the clowning can be self or other destructive. The mascot will often say outrageous things or confront serious issues by styling it with levity or even pseudo humor. Mimicry is a frequent mascot talent but may move into mockery. Much of their humor is self deprecating reflecting their shame and some of their humor involves put downs of others as a reflection of their anger. Sometimes the mascot is also a story teller, entertainer and teacher using fantasy and legend. The mascot may also be a caretaker, hoping to ease pain through humor. Other names for the mascot include distracter, clown, tension reliever, the family comic, mimic, charmer or court jester.

The Pleaser

Pleasers are nice and non-aggressive, usually following the path of least resistance. They tend to obey the rules and sometimes enforce them with other children but are careful about how they do the enforcing when adults are around. They are polite, well mannered, dress neatly and live for the recognition of perfect conformity. They tend to do well in various settings, figuring out what is needed for success and delivering it. Self motivation may or may not be present. If present, it is held in check until it is clear, it too, will please. Pleasers usually search out and suck up to the power centers in their work and are able to work within the system. The bind is they cannot please everyone. They may live life as if it were a popularity contest but they alienate some people. This alienation is a serious source of stress.

The pleaser does very poorly when they are in a bind of making choices where someone loses or will be hurt or angry. Pleasers have anger but are usually passive/aggressive, sideways or internalize it and self destruct. A pleaser may please the authority over them and then abuse persons they have authority over. There is a deep dishonesty inherent in the role. Persons with this role are hard to confront and it is difficult to maintain an honest or deep relationship with them. They may develop the classic codependent role of trying to be whatever the setting requires, give whatever is needed. Like a chameleon the pleaser may change colors and courses depending what is needed or expected. The absence of identity and self worth is the obvious source of their reactiveness to the needs of others and the molding of their definition of self by others.

Many pleasers do not have the anger. They are bright, sensitive, caring and please primarily out of their empathy for others and their need for connectedness. Other terms for pleasers are the good kid, placater, nice kid, model child, happy one. Descriptive words include quiet, pleasant, easy going, respectful. Pleasing is a form of care taking and enabling but is also the most effective way of surviving a mean system. Pleasers usually experience fewer incidents of abuse or rage. Eventually pleasers may become angry and move into the rebel or offender role, or experience physical symptoms and stress from trying to do it all and keep everything calm.

Surrogate Spouse

The surrogate is the child who is set up to nurture, notice, entertain or care for the needs of a parent. This role is discussed in bonding and enmeshment sections. Also called the confidant, best buddy, little prince or princess or daddy's girl or mommy's boy. May be the same gender of the over bonding parent or not.

Ma Bell

The family member other members communicate through but not to. "Tell your mother that . . . ," "go back and tell your father . . . ," "tell your sister to stop . . ." Sometimes using the person in the ma bell role is more subtle with nonverbal expectations of them passing the information on. The communicator often gets in trouble because of the 'kill the messenger' syndrome. Ma bell is triangulated by the indirect communication and can become the message center, the bearer of bad news, the informer, occasionally the organizer. Ma bell sometimes acts as the glue holding the family together through the dissemination of information, gossip, stories and changes. Other terms for ma bell include the informer, communicator, family link up, or in the 1990's the family internet.

The Rescuer

The rescuer drives an ambulance through life removing consequences and fixing things. With the rescuer around others maintain their irresponsibility by knowing they will be bailed out. This enabling role is generally played by the spouse of an addict or offender and often learned by the children. The rescuer engenders helplessness in others. It is a role of disrespect, not allowing others to face and deal with the consequences of their behavior. Other names for the rescuer are enabler, helper, fixer or healer.

The Dare Devil

Dare devils seek challenge and risk, living on the edge. They live by the slogan, "If you're not living on the edge, you're taking up too much space!" They are intensity junkies who cannot handle the normal flow, needing crisis and seeking distraction from their denial and fear. Dare devils often put others at risk in their thrill seeking.

They tend towards self destruction and have a difficult time with work and relationships, usually carrying a large load of barely repressed anger. In healthier systems the dare devil becomes the adventurer and explorer leading others to life enhancement through the modeling of risk. The dare devil is also called the thrill seeker, the 'crazy' one, and the wild one.

The Savior

One member of the family who attempts to save the family from destructive forces. They may crusade against excesses and attempt to counsel members into a new life. Sometimes a savior is so zealous about a new found quest they spend the majority of their time and energy dragging other members into the fold. The new quest may be religion, a health cult, recovery, a financial scheme or a new diet. Many work hard to compensate for the family by becoming involved in social solutions and healing processes, more of a compensator role. The savior is commonly rejected or avoided, often flipping from one cause to another, decreasing credibility but not fervor. Saviors frequently become evangelists and alcoholism counselors. The rest eventually sell insurance. Other terms for the savior role are crusader and rescuer.

Saint

The one in the family who remains good throughout the trials, often seemingly in another dimension of reality or 'above it all.' The saint may also follow a family script of sanctity by being abused and not complaining, by sacrificing self for others, by leading a hermitic or aesthetic lifestyle or by traveling the well worn path to sanctity called martyrdom.

Pollyanna

This is a blend of attitude and role. The role is one of naiveté and repression, the attitude is of eternal optimism and denial. Polly convinces self all is okay even as the family is crumbling. People do not have mental illness or addiction, they just have phases. Polly often interferes with efforts to get help by minimizing or completely denying the problem. They are quite happy and satisfied until the explosion of the family blows them away as well. Being naive and wearing blinders is very different than maintaining hope while accepting reality. Polly is an enabler.

The Family Sacrifice

A member who gives up their choices to care for the family, especially with aging, sick, impaired parents or occasionally a sibling or grand parent. This is a role parents play as well as children. They may enter the religious life or work for the vulnerable and under privileged. They may work themselves to death and even commit suicide to teach the family a lesson. They may give all they have to support other family members except their teaching is unnoticed, unappreciated and the sacrifice is all for naught. The family sacrifice is also called the martyr.

Nurturer

This child often adopts everything that lives, moves and breathes in the neighborhood - especially the wounded and orphaned. Unusually affectionate and loving toward people and other creatures, frequently not as good at taking care of self. Good at soothing troubled waters in turbulent times. Drawn toward teaching, nursing or helping professions until 'burn out' occurs. Often engaged in relationships with the walking wounded and severely impaired. Most nurturers do a great deal of enabling although in healthy systems they are a blessing and offer the essence of life to others. Other names for the nurturer are: healer, nurse, caretaker, placater.

Lady-killer/Man-killer

This is the boy or girl taught to achieve wants through seduction. Reinforced for sexual and manipulative behavior. Finds control and attention through such behavior and moves into acceptance by sexual conquest and using of others to achieve ends. It all seems quite cute in earlier years but is devastating to intimacy and sets up narcissistic and sociopathic behavior. This role often stems from the emotional incest dynamic. Other names for lady-killer/man-killer are charmer and seducer.

171

Tramp

Similar to lady killer but usually a female who is sacrificed in a role of being used, possibly turning dad or others on by being a script of fantasy. The child is overtly or covertly reinforced for acting out sexually or appearing 'as if.'

The Producer

The producer is the child or children who are taught their value is in work, what they produce will allow them to stay or bring virtue. They develop a work ethic at an early age and it becomes an attitude toward learning and earning. The producer works at everything including their play. They may become successful but not usually happy, evidence of a lost childhood. Another name for the producer is the worker.

Jeremiad

This is the child who continually forecasts doom and sees the end coming. The one who reflects the pathology in their view of life and sees the negative aspects only - of family, community and the planet. Jeremiads may be firm believers in the basic depravations of the human species and the ultimate destruction of our planet - sooner than later. Not much fun at parties but usually hangs in there with the family. Also known as prophet of doom or pessimist.

The Plain One

Not based on appearance as much as perception. Symptoms are low self esteem and dressing and grooming to match. Sometimes a contrast child for the family vanity or a counterpoint to an 'attractive' sibling or parent.

The Home Body

The child who never leaves. One who sees home as their refuge and refuses to enter the outside world. In the animal kingdom the more abused the creature the more difficulty in leaving the nest or lair. Home body may leave but returns, frequently taking care of elderly parents. Then they find a home of their own they seldom leave, though occasionally invite people over.

Orphan

Some children may feel like lost children because they did not have a place, but many feel more like orphans. Orphans believe they were picked up off the street, dropped in the corner of the living room and forgotten about from then on. They could not have been of this family, they must have been adopted or stolen. See also lost child.

The Defender

The one who defends the family members and the family system. The defender will protect to the point of denial and delusion and often reenact the system in their own life. Usually defensive to the point of enabling and unable to connect deeply with others. Healthy families do not need defending.

The General

The parent or child, usually a sibling parent who directs the functioning and direction of the family through orders or by leading. Generals take charge and have great power struggles with anyone with an idea or whoever defies them. Generals work out their strategy and tactics before the battle of leading the family. They may also focus on organization as the organizer.

The Antagonist

The family member who will turn everything and anything into a debate or argument. They often adopt postures they do not believe in, they are most disagreeable and usually too smart for their own good. They also are called the devil's advocate or great debater. The family experience is like a pre law degree for the antagonist. They begin most statements with "Yes, but . . ."

The Teaser

A parent or older sibling who pokes fun and teases as a facade for judgmental postures and cruelty. The teaser has one or more specific victims who they taunt to the point of distraction and even crisis. The teasing may look like intimacy but is really intended to avoid it.

The Queen Bee

The queen bee has everybody hovering, working and running around for them. They are bossy, demanding, distant and unable to offer support. They send the workers and warriors out so they can lay eggs.

The Gadfly

The gadfly is always buzzing around, noticing and prodding. They work toward change - sometimes positively, sometime destructively - but always buzzing. Often they are worker bees for the queen.

The Odd-Duck

Whatever is happening, they do it differently. They dress, act and work in an unusual way. It gets to be a repetition of sameness in how different they always try to be.

The Impostor

The impostor may be seen as competent but feel as through they are fooling people. They wear the clothing of adulthood and their vocation but feel lost in and disconnected from what they wear. A common role among professionals. The role has little to do with the level of functioning and the role may be present in high and low functioning families. The impostor is often seen in business suits and living with the fear that someone will expose them and see they are not as really competent as they appear.

The Historian

Chronicles the events, process and passages of family members and the family as a unit. May keep the history of several generations and is usually very anxious to talk about it. Generally is the first one in the family to own a video recorder and the only one who actually uses one.

The Social Director

Arranges family reunions, events, gatherings, games and adventures. Usually makes a great travel agent. The organizer is a similar role but has a compulsive need not just to organize social recreational events, but the family members lives, car pools, their death and your marriage.

The Voice Of Reason

The voice is even tempered with good timing offering a soothing influence when the heat is turned up. Acts like a sponsor or guide for floundering members.

Addict

Anything worth doing is worth doing fanatically. The addict will feel comfortable at any one of the two hundred different twelve step meetings offered. They even become compulsive about not being compulsive.

Forever Child

Charming, playful, endearing to all who come near. May be competent and gentle. Some integration of adult and child-ness, but the emphasis is on child.

Flower Child

The lover of all people and things. The flower child still lives with the peace sign and the sense of the communion of life, still vulnerable to marijuana dependency and searching for a commune that works.

The Politician

The politician sometimes sounds like the voice of reason but usually driven by ambitions and has a load of power issues, goals, and manipulations. They may be dishonest but generally get the job done.

The CEO

The CEO is the business director who helps members with financial advice and assistance, encourages retirement accounts, college funds, and usually has a tip or two for investments. Occasionally the tips even pan out.

The Athlete

Physically stimulating but very tiring to be around. Unable to simply relax with the company of others. Ongoing games of touch football, volleyball, skiing, hiking, golf and then tomorrow we will . . . .

Explorer

The explorer is Marco Polo with slides and stories. Seeks the unusual. Usually the only one who really knows the river that cuts right through town.

The Artist, Poet, Musician

Talented, sincere, entertaining, but generally poor. Quite difficult to hold a long conversation with since they do not watch sports or own stock.

Families may also have a philosopher, a healer, a baby sitter, an accountant, an attorney, a shopper, a maintainer, a klutzy or obnoxious one. Role labels involve the odd one, ugly one, dumb one, pretty one, smart one.

Destructive families teach destructive life roles. These may be based on the personal qualities of the individual, even an exaggeration of such attributes. They may be a product of the dysfunction or pathology of the family such as addiction, violence, neglect or denial. The roles have some relationship to adaptability, but little to character.

Frequently people identify with numerous role mentioned. This is adaptability to the extreme. Most of us have several roles and move from one to another. The roles mentioned above are by no means a complete list. Roles are as many and varied as systems and people are varied. Many family roles involve the loss of choice and identity.

Roles are difficult to give up or change because they involve habits and rituals, are based on beliefs and premises and can act as addictive processes. They involve how we view ourselves in the world, our mythology about us and our families, our learning, needs, feelings and personality. If we want to change our roles we must reevaluate basic world views and behaviors. We act roles out in every system we enter, our nuclear families, work, relation-ships, groups, committees, classes and communities. The roles become woven into lifestyle, changing involves unraveling the basic structure and reworking it, looking at each role and how they are interrelated.

The process of healing involves awareness of the old roles and learning new ones while keeping the strengths and positive aspects of the old ones. It requires replanting curiosity, thirst for awareness, and willingness to venture out on quests. These are the things often murdered in childhood. New roles can be dis-covered - the seeker, seeking awareness, seeking change, seeking becoming; roles of our spirit, inspiring ourselves and others to-ward a spiritual lifestyle; the role of guide and mentor, offering direction for others who have lost their way as we discover our life trail. New roles bring new adventure, deepening and enrich-ing the quality of the journey.

CHAPTER 17
Victim, Offender And Collusive Roles

There is no single incidence of violence as impact of Trauma.
The echoes of violence reverberate through our lives,
relationships, cultures, and families.
Echoes: Understanding & Resolving Trauma

In systems with abuse and violence there are three major roles around the abusive behavior - the victim, offender, and collusive. Members may move in and out of each of these roles or be in two at the same time but in abusive families, most members adopt one of the three roles as primary.

The term victim describes a Victim Role, not a person. It implies one is not responsible for what happened to them. The term survivor is often used in place of victim. The term survivor implies one is not responsible for what happened, and is taking responsibility for the solution, the resolution of what happened and for preventing it from reoccurring. One can move from the victim role into the survivor role over time in the healing process. Being a survivor does not discount the reality of having been a victim. Children who are victimized cannot be responsible for the resolution of their victimization or for protecting themselves. They need to be protected and guided in resolution.

Past victims may continue to get used and abused in present and future relationships. They are set up for random victimization outside of primary relationships and family. The random victimization can occur in childhood or adulthood. It can occur in part because the postures and style of the victim role become a magnet for offenders. Responses to the incidents of victimization include feelings of lost control over destiny, fear and a sense of being buffeted around by the winds of chance. Martyrdom and the inability to maintain healthy boundaries is common. Codependent styles of relationship and people pleasing are exhibited. Self care is difficult, taking care of others comes slightly more easily. In the victim role one may remain naive, not noticing their suffering except for the dull ache of repressed pain. In victims there is a tendency to block feelings of vulnerability, to hide the feelings of pain, hurt and fear that make one vulnerable. Effort is made to shroud insecurities and inadequacies behind false fronts hoping to prevent people from hurting or using them again. It may work but seldom fools offenders. The hiding of vulnerability only makes the healing more difficult. In blocking the vulnerability the victim will appear pseudo mature rather than naive, vulnerable or fearful.

The hidden fear becomes hyper-vigilance and produces free floating anxieties. Hyper-vigilance is the forever watchfulness, the state of constant alert and readiness for slights, hurts or intrusions. The anxieties float through life until they attach and become worries, frequently over attaching and becoming phobias.

The victim role itself is based on the residual aspects of traumas experienced, the past violence. Victims exhibit traits of codependency that are really aspects of post trauma stress reactions and disorders. Withdrawal, isolation, sexual and social inhibitions, insecurity, self destructive behaviors, disconnectedness, therapy distress, cynicism, loss of interests, personality collapse, memory loss, flat affect, mood swings, meaninglessness, low self esteem, impatience, defensiveness, depression are all reactions found in trauma sufferers. These earmarks of the role are symptoms of Post Trauma Stress Reaction.

The Secret

A person being victimized knows the abuse and violence in the family are to be kept secret. Their lives become controlled by both the secret, and why the secret is kept. *The secret keeping process can control one's life and relationships.* A victim of sexual, physical or other abuse knows if they talk about the abuse there will be consequences. They may be led to believe the consequences include being considered crazy by others and sent away. From then on their life and relationships are marked by the fear of any self disclosure, the fear of getting close to people because people will think they are crazy or send them away. Sometimes the reality is easier to deal with than the fear so the victim sets themselves up to be rejected. Sharing the secret or talking about the abuse brings increased fears of abandonment by the family. This fear of abandonment also causes a fear of intimacy and difficulty with self disclosure. The fear of abandonment from disclosure of the family secrets continues as fear of abandonment and self disclosure and fear of intimacy, for only with intimacy will the abandonment, hurt, or self disclosure occur. The secret keeping process is discussed more in *Family Gatherings*, Family Secrets chapter.

Victims set up distance, feel responsible, feel damaged and have very little trust in themselves. They tend to triangulate in relationships with other people, getting involved as a third party in other people's conflicts and needs. They may bear the burden of other people's problems and often establish a relationship with someone who is already in a relationship. This triangulation can bring about victimization by the other member of the triangle. In families with sexual abuse or inappropriate bonding the child is triangulated with the adults and tends to reenact the triangle in relationships, especially relationships with other offenders.

In the victim role, dissociation is a means of self protection. Dissociation is a splitting off of one or more aspects of self from the others. Victims split off the memory of past from present reality, feelings from awareness. They split off time, reality, affect, and personality. Dissociation may feel 'crazy' but is merely an elaborate defense mechanism, though often frightening and occasionally debilitating. The following is a list of dissociative responses.

- Feelings of Unreality.
- Depersonalization.
- Memory Loss.
- Multiple Personality Disorder.
- Mind Body Disconnection.
- Dream Repression.
- Affect Numbing.
- Feeling Crazy.
- Repression.
- Hallucination.
- Recurring Nightmares.
- Parallel Reality.
- Sociopathic Split.

Victims often feel hopeless and helpless experiencing fear and shame as controlling forces. They may not complain, becoming passively compliant to what ever life has to offer, no longer standing up for themselves. They often become a doormat with a passive posture toward life, bending to the will and whims of those around.

Relationships are difficult. If heterosexual, the tendency is to focus on other sex relationships ignoring the need for same sex nurturing and relationship. In childhood victimization, the same sex parent, even if they were not the abuser, was probably not available emotionally. The difficulties in other sex relationships partially stem from this absence of same sex nurturing, a key element in building a healthy relationship with oneself as a man or woman. Attempts to compensate with attention from the other sex fails, resulting in a series of empty conquests or a tendency to drive people away with neediness, or attract people who will use or abuse.

Victims are commonly self abusive, continuing the victimization cycle. The role is continued by physical or emotional self inflicted hurts and patterns of running away and avoidance. Victims of sexual abuse may practice 'inconspicuousness' as an art form. The ability to disappear and not be noticed is a primary defense. Victims of emotional abuse are set up to feel 'crazy.' In the emotional abuse the victim may not have the scenes to match the feelings. They often lack the specifics to process, making them feel less connected, 'crazier' or more disassociated. The emotional abuse itself may be crazy making, wrought with double messages, reality distortion, binds and conflicts.

Victims are not incapable of enjoying closeness, or enjoying sexuality, but frequently, especially victims of sexual abuse, will have a very difficult time having closeness and sexual intimacy together in the same relationship. Intimacy and sex become separate things.

Victims are attracted to offenders because they seem to possess what the victim lacks; assurance, confidence, aggressiveness, and strength. A victim will often make the first moves in building a relationship with an offender. This occurs in part to disarm the offender's power over the victim. Sometimes it is to get it over with, or to equalize responsibility for what happens. Victims keep trying to change people or the system so the abuse and the neglect will not continue. They did not set up the system and they usually cannot change it, they can only change themselves. The offending may continue as long as the offender or offenders have access to them. Even when terminating a relationship to avoid abuse or if the offender actually does change, until the victim role is resolved new victimization is set up or others found to continue the violence. Victims generally feel blamed and overly responsible for what is going on. There is a tendency in our culture to hold the victim responsible, to blame the victim. People blame the victim so they can view the victim as a loser, at fault or somehow different. This allows others to hold on to a belief in their invulnerability, it will not happen to them. Life is easier under the umbrella of invulnerability.

If the offenders took pleasure in inflicting the pain, or if they sexualized physical or emotional abuse, the victim role may involve a fusion of pain and pleasure. Pleasure is experienced in pain received, sexual acting out may become bondage and discipline or involve sadomasochistic rituals where pain is fused with the pleasurable experience.

Shame

The victim role is based on shame. Shame becomes internalized and grows into self-hate. It controls reactions and relationships. Since shame is tied into our relationship with ourselves as men and women all internalized shame becomes sexual shame. Because of their shame, the victims commonly attempt to bury sex as an issue. Sexual acting out is common, but developing healthy sexual relationships and holding good feelings about sexuality is difficult.

When feelings are held deeply and denied for long periods of time, the physical connection to the feeling, the sense of the feeling is lost. The shame may not be noticed until its messages of self hate and damaged identity become the basis of action and activity. Because of shame, other feelings are experienced as different and bad or not noticed or frozen. One is ashamed of other feelings which become a source or trigger for shame. When the shame is noticed it induces more shame.

The attempts to repair broken integrity or shame can become perfectionism. The unrealistic expectations of perfection cause a further shame response. In the process of the victimization the connection between punishment, behavior and consequences as well as our responses to the punishment or violence is lost. It becomes logical to believe punishment is meted out because there is something wrong with us. This self blame becomes a survival tool enabling functioning but disallowing full awareness of what may or may not bring on the punishment. Believing the problem is our behavior and not about the offender helps because if it has nothing to do with us, we feel too vulnerable and out of control. Eventually the self-blame helping us survive becomes a belief of brokenness spiraling into shame.

Fear

Victims commonly become fear based. Threats to survival places one on shaky ground. Growth requires safety, risk requires security. Many persons remain in hurtful settings because of the fear of leaving. Incidents of hurt are almost a relief because living with the fear of violence can be worse than the abuse. Anxiety disordered lifestyle prevents true being and living. The fear bond is often mistaken for love. The most important need is survival, when survival is threatened the ensuing fears and anxieties control.

Offenders are seldom consistent in their abuse, rage or punishing postures, so making a solid connection between behavior and consequences is difficult. The disconnection between the behavior and the punishment makes one feel 'crazy,' there is no figuring out why the hurt keeps happening or how to prevent it. The disconnection between the punishment or violence to behavior and losing the link to the responses to the violence causes the victim to develop a deep sense of being flawed, believing something is wrong with them. It is as though the problems in life are about who we are, rather than about what is happening or has happened to us.

Victims experience a loss of personal power and have a difficult time claiming or regaining it in relationships. Relationships with assertive, aggressive, offending persons may be a reenactment of the abuse and trauma from the past. Current physical, emotional and sexual intrusions are often the continuation of past boundary violations. Feeling powerless, the decision to leave is impossible, but if one relationship ends another offender can be found to continue the abuse.

The damage of sexual abuse is further internalized because sexuality is a core of identity. Victims of sexual abuse may develop a damaged goods syndrome. They feel broken in a way that seems impossible to repair. Victims frequently lock in on early incidents of abuse and repeat it, doing it to themselves or finding others who will hurt them in the same way. They keep trying to change who they are, what they do or say, but eventually go back to the same roles and patterns when discovering the changes do not work. There is terror involved in accepting there is absolutely no control over the abuser or over the events of violence. Accepting the only way to change it is by leaving or by calling for help is difficult. Within the role is a set up to allow the abuse to continue even though the victim is not responsible for the abuse happening.

The violence and feelings set up acting out. Compulsions, nasty mood inflictions, emotional swings, attempts to over control, and self destructive lifestyles may develop. The ability for self protection in other settings is lost and victims often hang around places where they are more likely to be hurt or re victimized. A tough veneer is put up. The defenses make it appear the abuse does not impact, but inside are isolated, frightened children. In recovery for victim issues, the 'crazy stuff' one does, needs to be connected to the victimization, the linking of the response to the violence. One must understand the responses are simply reactions to the abuse. The victim is not responsible for the abuse and is incapable of changing the abuser. It helps to see the situation as unique but not so unique that one feels too different and shameful. Knowing others have experienced similar things and have found recovery and intimacy is helpful. Learning to share the feelings helps healing. Looking at the rage and dealing with the fear of rage helps restore strength and outrage. Self gentleness and self forgiveness is best maintained while hanging around people who are gentle and affirming.

It is important in therapy not to role play the incidents of abuse. Going through them emotionally, verbally or physically will debrief the process and the incidents. In therapy sometimes the data and the feelings are disconnected. It is okay not to do the feelings work while looking at and talking about the events, or for others allowing the feelings to come for a time before talking and describing what happened. Eventually both must be done, the verbal and emotional debriefing, embracing and sharing the details remembered as well as the feelings experienced.

Victims need to learn being dependent is okay, and persons to depend on must be chosen carefully. Release comes from deep feelings or catharsis work. Feelings must be expressed as big as they are, not as big as we want them to be or think they are supposed to be. The deep emotional release must be done in safe settings and with moderation, not in large groups, but with guidance and support. Much of recovery involves learning to embrace and notice feelings in a mild way, linking self abuse with the abuse done and embracing feelings rather than trying to get rid of them. Care must be taken about swinging into offender roles. The secrets of the abuse must be told as well as how the secrets have controlled other aspects of life. Therapy involves new rules, roles, beliefs and premises. Realizing the absence of protection by our survival figures and others is painful but part of growth. It may not seem like they were abusive, but to not be protected by care givers is neglectful and abusive.

The victim does not have to face the offender. Often victims are told they must face the perpetrator to heal. This confrontation may be helpful or damaging and the decision must be made with care. Keeping distance may be more therapeutic. Being in the presence of the offender may be a continuation of the abuse. It is okay to set up the confrontation at some later point or not at all. Recovery is personal, not an attempt to change others.

The impact of abuse varies depending on who the offender is. Generally, the closer the abuser, the deeper the wounds. Sanctuary trauma, being hurt in safe places or by people who should be safe is the most difficult to resolve. An offender may be a parent, a family member, outsider, stranger, friend, teacher, neighbor, minister or counselor. Frequently when one is hurt by an outsider they do not feel safe enough to talk about it in family. Fear and pain is internalized and isolation results. The inability to express what has happened indicates the presence of neglect, shame or fear. Not feeling safe enough to talk about hurts is an earmark of an offending system. Random victimization stems from the victim role. The kind of abuse experienced outside of the family may reflect what was experienced overtly or covertly in the family. Offenders have a way of reading the victim, finding someone who has already been hurt, isolated, and has a difficult time defending themselves. They use or abuse the person with confidence, there will be few repercussions because the secret will be kept or the victim will blame themselves rather than the offender.

The victimization one remembers is usually the tip of the iceberg. More comes as one is ready to process it. *Therapy is not a search for memory. Memory is a by-product of the recovery process.* Memory loss is a protective measure but the hurts are never really forgotten, only the connection to how they are remembered is lost. The video image is not in the mind but the memories are stored in physical being as body memories and held in repressed feelings as emotional memories. Reconnecting with and noticing the physical self opens up past realities. Allowing the feelings, sounds, words, hurts tell of the past. The video image is not necessary, the need to trust the felt sense of what happened and allow the feelings to become healing is necessary. Working on building identity allows memory to flow. Memory tends to be evasive when pursued. *Searching for the reality of the past lessens the ability to find the reality of the past, for in the searching there is no finding.* One only has what is embraced. Embracing oneself offers reality - past and present.

Learning how to be vulnerable without remaining in the victim role is a part of recovery. Parents may not tolerate vulnerability in children because the vulnerability reflects dependence on the parent. Parents who are afraid of their children's dependency on them will beat or ridicule the vulnerability out of the child. Rediscovering and embracing vulnerability allows intimacy. Learning to feel guilt without getting flooded by shame can be followed by learning how to embrace the shame without it becoming a belief we are bad. Learning how to move from shame to a healthier sense of shame offers a sense of honor and guardianship. Accepting vulnerability allows one to cherish and protect vulnerability in others.

The impact of abuse is determined by several factors including the severity and frequency of the abuse and the age of occurrence. Generally, the earlier the age, the greater the impact. What is told or believed about the abuse, whether the abuse seemed to have meaning, the settings or context of where it occurred, the ability to talk about it after it happens and the ability to find confidants all impact the effect. This last issue is one of great importance. If one is able to talk about it close to the time of occurrence, much of the healing or therapy is done in this opening up and finding support. Most victims do not talk about it because of secret keeping enforcement. Many did not have anyone safe to share it with or were too ashamed or scared to talk about it. The period of time between the occurrence of abuse and the actual debriefing or talking about the abuse can determine the severity of the impact. Victims do move away from the victim role to become survivors, being responsible for the resolution and self protection. Victims have within themselves what is needed for the healing and the discovery of intimacy with self and others. Guides and support systems are needed to facilitate this healing process.

OFFENDER ROLES

Many victims bond, identify with and protect their aggressors. In this identification process, the victim learns to be the offender. An offender is usually a victim who is somehow enmeshed with a perpetrator. Victims feel bad about themselves, frightened and ashamed. They do not want to deal with feelings. Offenders get rid of their feelings at other people. Offenders are victims who cannot deal with the reality of their own victimization. They get rid of their feelings while hurting others with them. Offenders can use their shame to avoid their guilt, feeling badly about themselves but not their impact on others. The deep feelings of self hate get projected out towards others. Offenders often protect their parents or others who have hurt them and this protection flows into the denial of how they hurt people.

Offenders tend to lack impulse control, have a difficult time taking time outs and reasoning their way through emotional situations. They becoming hyper responsive to external and internal stimuli. They attempt to repress feelings and end up acting them out. Many offenders are 'rage-aholics'. They turn their pain, fear, shame and guilt into anger and lash out at others. Anger and the offending behavior acts as a release and mood alterant. Rage and abuse can be like a drug, not chosen but repetitively depended upon with a power to alter brain chemistry and offer emotional release and highs. These addictive rituals set up severe consequences for the offender and the victims. The anger leaves fear and distracts pain. It offers the illusion of power or control.

Offenders tend to feel and act like victims, believing they are being victimized in settings other than where the abuse really occurred in their lives. They may feel victimized by their present family, their spouse, the courts, therapists, the legal system and possibly the church and government. When it comes to dealing with their parents they may be in denial about any abuse or victimization. Even as offenders hurt others, they sometimes feel they are being victims in their offending behavior. The other person set them up or caused it and thereby deserves whatever they get.

There often is not a clear cut distinction between the victim role and an offender role. A person may be victimized in some settings but also victimizing others. In a relationship two people can seem to simultaneously hold both roles or very rapidly alternate roles in their victim and offending behaviors toward each other. One of the highest risk groups to hit children are battered spouses. Many people who offend are not in a primary offender role. They periodically lash out because of the feelings and dynamics of victimization but have not established a pattern of frequency and severity.

Offenders tend to minimize the impact of their behavior on others. They have a difficult time experiencing other people's pain as real. They minimize, project, transfer, and obsess. Offenders often do not like to know people are afraid of them so they ignore the fear in others. Some however, relish in the power coming from frightening people. Offenders may become alcoholics or other drug dependent, and some alcoholics become offenders. Usually the offending behavior is there before the alcoholism. In recovery and treatment the drug is usually blamed for the offending role but they are separate issues. The offender role and the rage sets up the alcoholism as often as the other way around. Many addicts are not offenders but some are. Some alcoholics drink and drive and others just get funny, pass out or isolate. While some want to shoot people or get into fights. The posture one practices depends more on the level of rage or offending behavior than the alcohol use. Alcohol however, does break down boundary sense and inhibition, the behavior of the alcoholic can become more offender oriented as the disease progresses. Drug use may link up with offending behavior and the link means both must be dealt with in treatment to facilitate recovery in either. The possible addiction to the offending behavior as well as the addiction to drugs must reviewed. When only one issue is treated it generally resurfaces and a double helix forms. With some drug problems the individual is automatically enveloped in criminal and offending behavior. The need to keep a supply or source sets up repetitive criminal behavior.

Offenders can be charming, likable, seductive and controlling. The rage they project at others often a misdirection of their rage at parents or others from their past. Offenders have a difficult time profiting from experience. They have trouble grieving and feeling remorse and are frequently obsessive and paranoid. The intrusiveness, ability to control, defend, rationalize and manipulate can make them attractive to victims. These are 'qualities' missing in the victim role. Offenders' primary defense postures are transference, projection, and minimization. They can become rageful or attack a person because they remind them of someone else in their life. They act out their past trauma experiences by reenacting the trauma itself. Only in their reenactment do they feel power.

A symptom of post trauma effect often seen in offenders is sensation seeking, an addiction to intensity. There is a tendency to be controlled by arousal responses-rage, resentment, agitation, impatience, arousal, and anger. Other primary emotional responses to earlier traumas are anxiety reactions leading to fear, paranoia, obsessing, hyper vigilance and startle responses. These fear states are more threatening and reflect loss of power, thus the more powerful arousal states are used to cover anxiety and terror. The offending eases symptoms of post trauma reaction but in the process can cause more trauma and more symptoms. Offending behavior itself is a post trauma stress disorder symptom. The violence in the lives of the Viet Nam vets, law enforcement officers and others who work with violence and aggression can be a reflection of the unresolved past trauma issues in their lives. The work reenacts this past traumas setting up more symptoms. Law enforcement, military and emergency personnel sometimes move into offender roles, acting out the arousal symptoms from the witnessing of and experiencing trauma in their work.

Offending behavior is multigenerational. Offenders are created by offenders. A family system where offending takes place has to have victims. This is one reason why a family might adopt or take in foster children or animals and become very abusive towards them. One would imagine that anyone who would voluntarily take in a child or adopt a pet would never hurt the child or pet. The offender needs the victim, a vulnerable creature for their projected feelings. Under the guise of caring they place the child or pet in the victim role. Most people who care for children do so out of love and concern, but not all. They may not be consciously aware they are taking the child in to victimize.

Tremendous harm can be done to family members without consequences to the one doing the harm. Many abusive behaviors in families are behaviors that would be prosecuted by law if attempted on someone outside the family.

Offenders often come from rigid, paternalistic systems, especially sex offenders. There are usually dominance and submission issues in their relationships. Male sex offenders generally have issues with power and rage. The offending system often rests on a substructure of woman hate. They may come from highly religious families with sexual repression. They act out a compensatory masculinity, not feeling like they fit the cultural image of a real man, the 'Marlboro Man' with horses nuzzling the ear, smoking a cigarette, wearing cowboy boots, leaning against a split rail fence with women falling at their feet. Since they cannot act this out in the culture, some try to compensate in their own families.

When the offender sexually abuses they tend to blame the victim. Incest fathers will build supporting fantasies and claim they fell in love, romanticizing the incident or seeing invitation, seduction, acceptance where none existed. They frequently find excuses and blame the offending on marital problems, work pressure or some other issue. They act out rituals of control and seduction even when not actively engaged in the battering or sexual abuse, becoming as addicted to the rituals of the offending as to the acts of the offending. Many offenders are extremely sensitive to their fears and anger. When they experience their own emotional reality they tend to take it out on others. The impact of violence on children and spouse is minimized by both the offender and the spouse or partner.

Issues to resolve include the lack of impulse control, the impact of behavior on others, learning healthy guilt and a sense of shame without falling into complete self hate. They must talk about and debrief the offending behavior and gradually work into how and where they were victimized, doing the emotional and cognitive debriefing of past hurts. Self help support groups and twelve step programs can be helpful, but offenders also need to be a part of facilitated process with strong leadership, lots of support, firm limits and boundaries.

Separating offenders from their victims is important to protect the victim and gives the offender a better chance for recovery. Eventually recovery from offending roles requires looking at the victim roles. In offenders, the two roles are intertwined. Offenders also need to face and hear stories of victims but initially do better hearing it from victims they have not hurt.

The offending can become an intensity addiction where the past pain and hurt are shrouded by the intensity and passion of the experience. As the rush of the intensity wears off the fear, shame, and pain resurface and the cycle repeats.

COLLUSIVE ROLES

The third primary role of the violent system is the collusive or enabling role. Collusion occurs when one is not being directly abused or doing the abusing but is around or involved with others who are and do not recognize, prevent, or report it. The collusion is usually the role of the spouse or partner to the offender. Parents of violent children also collude as do children who enable and learn to tolerate the violence around them. The collusion can be active or passive. Active collusion is done by a person who is involved in the victimization and knows actively what is happening. They may be glad it is happening, get off on it, or simply be relieved it is not them being victimized. They will not report the victimization and may show a lack of interest in changing things, often intentionally doing what will trigger incidents.

Passive collusion is done by the person who is unaware the victimization is going on or feels helpless and powerless about what to do. They often wear blinders. The blinders are usually worn because of the severity of abuse experienced or witnessed in their own history. The collusive person usually has an altered baseline tolerance level for abuse because of this past abuse or violence. Though they collude, the spouse is also the most likely person to report sexual abuse when they have the information.

The spouse of the offender may seems 'crazier' or sicker than the perpetrator although they seldom are. They can look hostile, depressed and very out of touch, operating within a parent child role reversal. The collusive adult often acts like a child while the children in the system act more like adults frequently giving advice, nurturing and support to parents. The enabling spouse may eel and take the blame but will abdicate responsibility. Their self blame spirals into self pity. The primary defenses are denial, rationalization and introspection. Collusives refuse to look at the impact of what is going on, not sensing the full reality of it. They make excuses and do a great deal of personal soul searching without really changing. They become more withdrawn and obsessed with self. The collusive partner has a difficult time setting limits on themselves or others and may be very compulsive and progressively lose impulse control. They are afraid to stand up to the offender and when they do, they do so in a way that may escalate the violence. When the offender acts out the collusive person might see their part of the escalation as 'getting even' or 'justice.' They carry and internalize resentment and rage. While acting childlike they still try to hang on to their power which they wield covertly through manipulation. They can seem uncaring, critical, neglectful and competitive. When children are being victimized, they may look at the children and think, "Better you than me," or the belief may be subconscious level.

The collusive spouse role is difficult to evaluate. They may care so much they get helpless. They sometimes feel so much pain about what is going on they become over controlling, rageful and offending themselves. Sometimes they get in the way of the abuse to the point of getting hurt or are afraid to get in the way because the abuse may escalate. They often come from violent backgrounds of abuse and neglect. They carry immense anxiety sensing something is wrong but ignorant of what it is or how to deal with it.

People in the collusive role may experience unwanted conflicting emotions setting up a pattern similar to the offender's, *to get rid of feelings rather than embrace, feel and share them.* They may become narcissistic, caught up in their own pain or can become enmeshed in the pain of the offender. They assume the enmeshment is love and understanding but it is really enabling. They often blame or resent the victim and deal poorly with the reports of abuse, responding with disbelief or, "Why didn't you tell me sooner," or some other offender protective statement or neurotic escalation.

This role requires a realistic assessment of the damage done by the collusion in the context of background and choices. Most persons in the collusive role have been hurt deeply in their past and need to understand the link of the past hurts to present reality and helpless postures. They attach old fears and hurts to current relationships and family, thereby keeping old issues buried while recreating them. They believe it can happen to anyone and it is a random occurrence happening to them. They do not see their part in facilitating violence and do not easily accept they are choosing the relationship with the perpetrator. Their self blame and shame breeds hopelessness and helplessness rather than responsibility and resolution.

People in collusive roles need to be affirmed for what they have tried to do and shown what they did not do. While learning they are not responsible for the offending behavior, they must accept how they hurt their children by not protecting them or dealing with their needs.

Collusives are extremely codependent and often addicted to intensity and crisis, and are seduced by power. In the spouse role there is a great range of motivation and personality. It is important to do judicious evaluation and look at the particular issues and background without blaming. They tend to vacillate between feeling responsible for everything and feeling as though none of it is their fault. They need to take the responsibility that is theirs and assign the responsibility that is not.

Past violence alters one's tolerance for violence it may either sharpen sensitivity to violence or dull it. Of the three roles around violence, the collusive role is the most common. Most persons are not actively being violated or actively hurting others, but many collude with violence, in the culture, cities, on the streets, the violence of war, rape, poverty, the homeless, the violence towards vulnerable people in our culture, even the violence done to the environment. Family violence causes a collusion with the cultural and planetary violence. Collusion is the primary codependent role and the basis for an offender protective system and inappropriate family loyalties. It is also the basis for incarcerating rather than rehabilitating offenders thereby continuing the offending system. Changes will come when enough people accept the true impact of the reverberating consequences of violence. *There is no single act of violence. Violence produces echoes spiraling into social systems, families, culture, relationships and environment.* The call is to rise above past violence and find the strength to alter the course of the offending on all levels.

The victim, offender and collusive roles each involve compulsive repetitions of past violence, experienced and witnessed. Resolution of past violence and trauma is essential to break free of the roles.

CHAPTER 18
Birth Order Roles
Wait In Line

On the day of your birth the tides washed the beaches clean of all previous markings in preparation for your footsteps.

On Eagles Wings

Most discussion of birth order is based on the theory developed by Alfred Adler on First, Middle, and Last Born. The following theory is based on a model developed originally by Jerry Bach and Alan Anderson. *As with all role description and theory the following describes tendencies and possibilities not rigid rules governing behavior.* The following is a construct of noticing and ideas rather than scientific fact.

ORDINAL POSITION

How one operates may be based partly on how and when they enter the family system. In social systems there are four basic functions or needs to be taken care of that follow in order. The first is *productivity*. A system does not survive without it. The next need is *maintenance*, primarily emotional but also physical such as tending to the children or the vulnerable people in the system. The third need is *relationship*, each aspect or member relating to the other. The final need of the system is for *wholeness*, the unity and accomplishment of group goals in the system. These needs are hierarchical in order. The first need is the first need. When all four of these system needs are recognized and met, members of the family function and operate as a healthy family unit. The children are allowed to be children and not placed in adult roles. The adults can enjoy their functioning as adults while incorporating a sense of childness. In a lower functioning system where issues of productivity, maintenance, relationship and unity are over stressed or not provided by appropriate persons, the family members react. Adults in the system have the primary responsibility for fulfilling these functions. When the parents abrogate responsibility because of addiction, illness, stress, carelessness, emotional immaturity or for whatever reason, children generally became overinvolved in these four aspects of family functioning.

As children are born into the system, they tend to identify with these needs in the order they are born. Thus, first borns identify more with productivity issues, seconds with maintenance, thirds with relationship and fourths with unity and wholeness. When one child reacts to a need, it's as though the next child reacts to and is assigned the next need until all four needs are met. If more children enter the system, the entire process tends to repeat itself. Thus a fifth may become more like a first, a sixth follows the patterns of a second, etc. The four system needs are the reason writers in the past have referred to the four primary child roles in family systems. This 'four role view,' however, is an oversimplification and stereotypical scripting. There are many roles in a system as well as many needs. *This birth order theory is not meant to be descriptive of people, rather a discussion of systems, viewing cause and effect and the interaction of aspects of the system.* There are other factors besides the systems needs affecting birth order role - first borns will have different pressures than last borns. The middle children react not just because of the number child but also the juxtaposition between other children. Again, a breakdown in adult role functioning causes children to role play for family functioning and personal security. These attempts can cause anxiety, stress and inadequacy. When the family functioning disintegrates individuals lose their ability to meet personal needs or build boundaries and identity.

Ordinal position theory is a systems theory not a trait theory. Describing ordinal roles is like describing the wind. The wind in the desert is very different than the same wind going through a city or a forest. We do not describe the wind, but rather the effect the wind has on what the wind passes through. With ordinal position theory we do not describe the individual but rather the impact of the birth order of the individual in regards to the particular system. The impact will vary depending on other roles, issues, personalities, settings and family dynamics. What is true for a first born in one family is not going to be the same for the first child in another. However, the way first children react to differing elements in family may have some similarities because of being first. Different systems dictate different needs and impact children in different ways.

FIRSTS

The first need is productivity, insuring the survival of the system. Survival is the real need, and the survival needs set up productivity responses. Any child may focus on issues of productivity for various reasons but the first child more often takes it on as a primary issue. In this culture fathers have traditionally been in charge of productivity so the first child may react more to the father's system and responsibilities, met or unmet. First kids may have equally strong feelings about both parents but their identity is more about who the father is. They may be close to Dad or not but they generally react to him. They often defend the father and become an extension of him. They may also take an opposing stance, for example, if Dad is an overachiever the first child may become an under achiever. The first child may not be close to Dad, but will be the most likely to fill in if Dad is missing or somehow needs help in maintaining his position in the family. Firsts are often driven to achieve, handle responsibility and produce. The particulars such as gender, specific limitations and personality effect how the first reacts to productivity. A first may be irresponsible but even the irresponsibility issues circle around productivity.

All systems have overt and covert rules. First children are more likely to support and enforce the overt rules. This stems from their patriarchal like responsibilities in the system as well as the amount of time parents spend with the child on overt training and being very clear about rules. Parents are usually more specific with the first and teach in pieces or by the book while focusing on rules, should be's and how to's. The first child gets tied in more with learning and achieving to build an identity. They often get frightened and anxious if rules, directions or processes are not explicit enough. They need to know the rules and structure to function securely.

Firsts often have a difficult time enjoying and flowing with the processes of life. They may get depressed if not active and seem to have a need to be into projects. They experience a hard time just 'hanging around' often feeling they have not done enough or are not doing enough. They believe they are going to be judged by how much and how well they have done and have an ongoing competency hearing going in their heads. When the jury comes back it is usually with the verdict they did not do enough or it is a hung decision. Firsts believe they are going to be cared about or loved for what they do rather than for who they are. Their family position will often uphold or react to Dad's position. If the system of the first child is looked at closely, it will usually reveal Dad's true premises, beliefs and style. If the first child is female they may try to become the kind of woman Dad would want a woman to be. This may or may not be like Mom. If Dad is absent they relate to the fantasy of Dad or other men. If Dad is absent the first tends to fill in his place, when Dad returns there can be a period of competition loaded with resentment. If Dad disappears and does not return and Mom remarries, the first may become depressed or defiant having lost their job and resist the intrusion.

The first child's energy frequently revolves around power issues. In systems they tend to feel responsible and powerful. They respond to power and easily engage in power struggles. If there are preexisting power struggles in the family, especially within the marriage, or with the marriage partner's parents, the first child will likely either uphold Dad's position or react against power and avoid power struggles to the extent of acting and feeling powerless.

They generally perform well but are vulnerable to performance anxieties. Excess expectations will cause them to try harder until it is impossible, then they defy. One of the hardest things for a first child to hear is that someone is disappointed in them.

In functioning it seems they need to have all the pieces, but they often miss the relationship between the parts. Parents teach their first children in pieces. This is a cup, this is chalk, this is a chalk board. In schools, where teaching is done in pieces, first children may do very well. In the world, math, science, biology, astronomy and history are not separated or separable. Only in school is this possible. First kids do better at the separation of the process of learning than the integration. When the later children come along in the system they learn more in concepts or from the older children. The pains are no longer taken to teach in the same way as the first. The third child is told to get their own cup of water, rather than what a cup is or what water is!

First children often seem as if they are out of touch with their feelings and less responsive to instinct. Given a chance they can reach their feelings, just a little more slowly. First children are more task oriented and may have a difficult time showing feelings. They have more rules, should have's and ought to's about their feelings. They tend to take in information on a cognitive level and then gradually down into the feelings with time and support.

Primary life issues include looking for external validation, being over protective, irresponsible versus over responsible and power seeking. They frequently play the little parent, hero and caretaker roles. They have a problem with the vagueness of concepts like codependency recovery issues. In organizations they try to figure things out and fix them, feeling responsible for all that is going on around them. In a family with an absent, dysfunctional or alcoholic father they feel the loss and try to fill in but they do not like to deal with their pain, tending to internalize it while adopting a defiant stance. They frequently have security and financial fears tying into their productivity issues.

If Mom is missing or alcoholic, the first may fill in to protect Dad from the humiliation or the additional responsibilities. They often develop a pattern of disliking or not trusting women. First children need to feel adequate, that what they do is enough, and to like themselves for who they are not what they do, to relax without being project or production oriented. If the first scrutinizes their beliefs, values, and life systems, Dad's will usually be revealed. They need to be careful of power struggles and over responding to expectations, while learning to see the relationship between the parts and pieces. It is helpful for firsts to give themselves time to feel. First kids may be very socially aware while frequently struggling with self esteem. In teaching and therapy situations it is important to emphasize clarity and do process including insight. Things must make sense. Talk therapy is easiest for firsts but they also benefit from imagery and non verbal emotional work.

SECONDS

Since the first need of productivity is the arena of the first child, the second child attaches to the second system priority, the maintenance needs of the family, especially emotional maintenance. These include noticing and caring for persons in the family who hurt or need the most, and tending to the daily functioning while maintaining the covert rules. The first child operates out of the overt, the second out of the covert or the family unconscious. They usually do not know what to label or how to explain what they uphold. Seconds

211

take charge of the covert rules, the unspoken, often unnoticed messages governing behaviors and lifestyle. There are covert rules about feelings, sex, touch, relationships, communication, lifestyle and so on. Seconds feel the problems, tension or fear of the family usually before anyone else does. They get caught up in the feelings but miss what the feelings are about. They can feel terrible but not connect the feelings to the cause. Perhaps the family dog dies or their best friend moves away, they will have feelings about it, but miss the link. The second child will notice what they feel, but will not always notice why.

Seconds tend to react to unconscious patterns in the world - destructiveness, defensiveness, alienation. Subsequently they tend to pick up more fear because they do not make these unconscious connections explicit. In sensing the covert reactions of people they frequently ascribe malevolence to others where none exists. A second will react to the anger or sour mood of a friend possibly before the friend has noticed it. They may believe the mood is about them when in fact it has nothing to do with them. Seconds often try to explain too much because they have less ability to label or summarize. A second entering a system with much hidden anger will react to the anger, usually with anger of their own. In attempting to take care of it they may over explain, often exacerbating the problem, rather than being able to sum up what happened and what they went through. The explanations offered can be a continuation of the problem. Second children can be very competitive and often notice what is missing in the system, what does not feel right. In their reactiveness to hidden issues and feelings they tend to follow emotional ups and downs and operate in extremes. They may be very up or very down, very close or very far away, very funny or very serious.

Seconds tie in to Mom because women in our culture have been in charge of emotional maintenance, feelings and hurts, as well as the physical maintenance of family. Very often their relationship with Mom is distant or angry but the second will still defend her. In our culture Moms often have anger or pain about their lives and what they give up for others. A second child reacts so intensely to the anger or pain they have a difficult time getting close to Mom. The distance and anger in the relationship between Mom and the second may become overt but the emotional connectedness is still present so wanting to defend mom's position also remains.

In groups seconds often get engrossed in the feelings to the extent of having a difficult time functioning. To protect themselves, they may move to the opposite posture, of totally ignoring feelings. They have a difficult time working in the middle areas, tending to operate in extremes.

A male second child may have a strong male identity but will identify with mom as well. They need both male and female bonding including permission to be close to women. Seconds may feel confused because no one talks about what the second notices. In our culture people do not often talk about what they are really feeling. When angry with a second it is important to let them know you also care about them because they become so reactive to anger, even unexpressed anger. Confrontation must be gentle and honest since the second will sense how you feel and easily believe you do not like them. Shame and anger are common responses to evaluation. They easily respond to parent's low self esteem, especially Mom's and often internalize it as their own. The shame becomes a belief system founded on self hate rather than the feeling of shame.

Problems stem from:

- Getting emotionally enmeshed with others.
- Attempts to make everybody feel okay.
- Being overwhelmed with feelings.
- Overreacting to covert rules without knowing where the rules came from or what they are about.
- Operating in extremes.

If Dad is absent, dysfunctional or alcoholic, seconds tend to be protective of Mom and more hostile towards Dad and men. They react to and act out Mom's feelings. They feel helpless and power-less, a traditional codependent stance. If Mom is absent, low func-tioning or alcoholic, they tend to protect the image of mom, deny the problem or try to fill in for her. They will sometimes internalize the self hate and helplessness of Mom. This may also develop into a woman hate system. Seconds who are girls will reflect Mom's sys-tem even though they often do the opposite of Mom. Second boys may try to be the kind of man Mom would want a man to be, unless they have been scapegoated or neglected severely and then they rebel but still operate in the paradigm of Mom's image of men.

Seconds will act out unconscious expectations and have a difficult time connecting their feeling and thinking awareness. They may seem puzzled. In therapy they respond better to fantasy, role playing, psycho drama and cognitive/affective models. They need to develop a sense of security and accep-tance about emotional issues. Seconds may feel 'crazy' early in treatment because they feel the feelings without having the labels and awareness about what they feel.

THIRDS

The third need, relationship, becomes a focus of the third child. They tie into the relationship issues of the family and operate in terms of connectedness. Since the most important relationship in a family is the marriage, the third child often reflects the quality or style of the marital relationship. They also get preoccupied with establishing balance in the family, tending to react to conflicts by distorting the elements to make things even. If one parent yells at the other, and the other responds by hitting, the third child will perceive it as being even though not equal. The third often sees both sides of a conflict and becomes paralyzed, not knowing how to deal with the conflict. A third may get angry at generalizations but often generalizes to keep connected. They frequently defend or bond more with the parent who is overtly hurting the most. They have a difficult time dealing with people who are objective and detached and believe people have to know them well before they can decide what kind of relationship distance they should have. They want to be understood before the other person decides on a relationship. Thirds generally like people who like them. If they are treated well they assume the relationship is good whether it is or not. If treated poorly, they may stil remain to protect the relationship. They often live as though life is a popularity contest.

Anger and loneliness in the parent's marriage is often reflected in the third child's life. They act out the style and conflicts of the parent's marriage. In families where the marriage partners are not close the family may react by not getting clse or bonding to the third child. The third child tries to be likable because they are relationship oriented, often attempting to fix or maintain the relationships of others, but miss taking care of their own relationships.

Thirds have a tendency for ambivalence. They have difficulty with choices, seeing both sides of the issue. Choosing one thing is a choice against all the other possibilities. When offered too many choices thirds will feel stuck or overwhelmed. They also change their minds and alter choices rather easily. In relationship they connect, disconnect and then come back again. They do not do well with direct confrontation and usually need process time to accept criticism. They have a difficult time seeing their parents as separate individuals, viewing them more as a couple and easily getting trapped in the sense of failure around the marriage. In single parent families the third child may fill in for the missing parent if the position hasn't already been taken. They still reflect the single parent's relationship issues including the past and present relationship with the missing partner.

Thirds improve their self concept when they see it as a relationship with themselves. Their life issues include a tendency to give up themselves to make relationships work. They often have difficulty with their identity, losing who they are in relationship with others. They easily become overly reactive, setting themselves up for trouble by trying to fix the relationships of others. They over respond to how people feel about them and may have less sense of self and more identity diffusion problems, losing themselves in different ways in different systems. Sometimes they stay detached because of the fear of losing too much of themselves. They will only put their toe in the water. They may not take the risk to dive in and work for intimacy.

Their emptiness or hostility is often a reflection of their parent's relationship. If their parents have a lazy, angry marriage the third child may feel the laziness or anger within themselves and act it out. If the father is dysfunctional, absent or alcoholic, they tend to bond with and take care of Mom while trying to fix things. If Mom is alcoholic, dysfunctional or absent they will tend to bond with and protect Dad while also taking care of Mom. Third kids may seem uninvolved but really are. They have a difficult time making choices and establishing separate identity but their concerns are still about relationship. In therapy and treatment it is important to focus on their feelings about relationships and to talk about relationship building. It is also important to deal with identity building and decision making. They need help to find a sense of separateness or detachment so they can take risks in life and relationships. Their attachment issues easily become codependent relationships or relationship addiction. They respond best when they feel cared about.

FOURTHS

Fourth children tend to be keepers of the system. The fourth system need is unity and wholeness so they tend to be absorbed in the system as an entity. Fractured families can drive fourths to the wall. The fourth feels responsible for the entire system and usually feels powerless to do anything about it. An image might be Atlas with the world on his shoulders, carrying it around, holding it up but not being able to effect change, feeling the pressure of what can one do with the world back there?

Fourths usually understand much about each member of the family as well as the whole family. They uphold the main universal truths and overall family system in their values and reflect these in their reactions and expressions. They keep the premises and reflect the flavor of the family. The blend of power and helplessness often keeps them stuck and causes problems with their own competency. They tend to view things in global terms but often miss details. Fourth children receive as much parenting from other children as parents so they learn differently and have fewer details. They see the family as an entity with some of the data missing. They believe they have the whole picture and thus have difficulty accepting the pieces they have not included. Their picture is like swiss cheese.

When there is responsible leadership in the family they do very well. If there is no leadership they flounder and act out. They can be emotionally expressive but often it is like steam off a kettle. They prefer to avoid going into deeper feelings.

Fourths make strong commitments and become good group members. They tend to be very involved with their group especially if the group has a strong sense of purpose and leadership. They also make good mimics because it is how they learn. Anyone in the family can learn to be a clown and relieve tension but fourth kids have an edge on the others. They blend the ability to imitate or mimic with awareness of the deep issues and sensitive areas of the family. Many fourths are very serious. They frequently are stuck because their premises about the world may be false. Low functioning families operate with many false and 'crazy' premises and premises are important to fourth children.

The fourth is often considered the garbage collector of the family. They collect the needs, roles, dilemmas, hidden pathology, thought disorders, etc. that do not get resolved or dealt with by other family members. They then try to figure out what to do with it. Whatever is not hooked up or acted out by anyone else in the family falls to the fourth.

Goals are very important. They will tend to achieve or get there if the goals are clear. Without goals they wander. Their major problem is becoming enmeshed in and sacrificing themselves for the system, then floundering with a lack of direction. The fourth is easily led by someone who seemingly has answers for them, often they are led astray. They may feel and act helpless.

A favorite fourth child story occurred on a wilderness trip in northern Minnesota with a group of adolescents who had been through addiction treatment and were living in a halfway house. On this canoe trip during one of the longest portages an adolescent girl was carrying a large seventeen foot canoe, whimpering, crying, complaining and driving everyone 'crazy.' One of the instructors came up to her and said, "Cindy, it hurts to carry a canoe, especially if you are not used to it. This is the longest portage of the trip. We are going to go about seventy-five yards along this path, then it veers off to the right and we go up a hill for fifty yards then we go down a gradual decline of 100 yards, and over a small ridge, then the path drops down to the lake where we turn the canoe over, get in and the canoe carries us to our campsite on the other side of the lake." The instructor dropped back and suddenly Cindy began whistling and singing to

herself. Of course the others began to whimper and cry and complain because they did not want to know how long it was going to be!
They could handle the portage one step at a time but it turned out to
be much longer than they expected. Cindy, however, knew where
she was going, she had her goal in mind and she knew explicitly she
could manage the pain. She felt much better.

If Mom is dysfunctional, absent or alcoholic, fourths will often
have a very poor self image and easily become the scapegoats of
sibling abuse and teasing. When Dad is dysfunctional, absent, or
alcoholic, and there is no leadership in the family, no decision making, the fourth experiences deep security fears. They will flounder
and become extremely anxious. Fourth kids tend to react to and
identify with all the interactions in the system and feel stuck between
the responsibility and powerlessness. An articulate fourth child can
describe the entire family system in detail. They may appear infan-
tile or immature because they are often treated in a baby like fashion
by other siblings.

In treatment it is important to look at what they are good at and
help them develop a sense of mastery and competency. They need
coping skills and goal setting. Behavior modification tends to be
effective. As they develop competency they give up their helplessness and accept responsibility for own behavior and their impact on
their relationships and lives. Healthy leadership, modeling and explicit clarification of goals are important.

*Sally was very competent and fiercely independent. She
portrayed a tough, sometimes hostile posture and never felt
like she fit in. In fact, she was repetitively doing things and
structuring her life so she wouldn't fit in. She also felt very*

stuck in her life and relationships. This 'stuckness' was erod-
ing her competency and marriage.

An exploration of her toughness and anger exposed her
fear. Sally was afraid of losing herself, of not being important.
She had just borne her first child and feared having to give
up her needs, the same fear she had about her marriage. Her
angry posture not only covered her fear it enabled her to battle
the forces that would have her lose 'herself.' The problem
was she was stuck between the fear and the anger and needed
to deal with either one to become unstuck.

Sally realized in therapy much of her need for indepen-
dence, her 'human doing' approach to life came through her
mother who in her mid 1970's was working full-time and po-
litically involved. Women had to work harder to have recog-
nition and value.

Sally was the fourth child of five. She said she was al-
ways refusing to do things with her family, her first experi-
ence in believing she did not fit. In her childhood she felt like
she did not belong at school, had few friends and often felt
left out or refused to join. When her family was on a trip or
outing she stayed back. She believed this was her indepen-
dence and uniqueness, and built a belief system around it.

She was shocked to discover as a fourth child she was
doing a very good job of reflecting the system. It was really
the family itself that did not fit in as a Protestant intellectual
family living in a Catholic blue collar neighborhood. The
family members even felt like they did not fit in at the beach,
on vacation, in their interests, the kind of car they drove, or

how they kept the lawn. Mom would repetitively announce, "We do not want to lower ourselves to fit in."

Both her parents were successful misfits. Sally's reaction to the family was not a way to independence, it was a reflection of the family system. She upheld the family values, system, and traditions in her work, relationships, defensiveness, and sabotaging of the possibilities of belonging and community. She came from a system of competent, hostile defiance based on fear, and it was not working for her. Her belief of being unlike her family kept her from seeing herself as the bearer of the system caught in a life not of her making.

ORDINAL POSITION SUMMARY

Since the system has four primary needs as more children enter the family these four issues are recycled. The fifth, again, tends to attach to productivity issues while the sixth ties into maintenance and so on. In our culture we are seeing fewer third and fourth children which may create a loss of relationship and unity for us with an over focus on productivity, individuality and emotional expression.

Difficult issues for first children are responsibility and unconditional self acceptance. Father loss or betrayal can be important recovery issues. The lack of healthy modeling by men must be processed. Seconds have issues around feelings, self worth and moderation. Mom's pain and pathology are often recycled through seconds and in recovery the attachment or betrayal by Mom becomes important, although the second will often feel they are betraying Mom. Thirds have a difficult time with decisions and loneliness. Therapy

222

issues include dealing with the problem in or the lack of parental relationship. Thirds are often enmeshed in several relationships. Fourths need to deal with helplessness and create healthy goals.

Ordinal position theory is a view of the family from one angle. It does not spell out absolutes but offers general themes to assist in understanding. Approaching systems theory in this manner may help clarify current life issues. It does not make things change. How one enters a family is only one aspect of role identity. Ordinal position can be important in how it interacts with other issues such as other roles, personality and family dynamics. *Ordinal position is not a descriptive theory but a systems theory.* Remember, describing the effects of birth order on an individual within a system is like describing the wind. Second children in different families may be very different because they are reacting to so many different circumstances. What we learn from understanding our roles in the system including birth order roles can help us make decisions for change. Nothing changes until it becomes real. Recovery involves debriefing the system the family operates by.

ONLY CHILDREN, BLENDED FAMILIES & OTHER CIRCUMSTANCES

Only children are often bonded with or become extensions of both parents. They may play out additional roles in the family because no one else is available to do it. This does not mean they take on all the roles. Only children are first children. They do tend to socialize differently, leaning more towards socializing with adults than with their own peer group. They also tend more towards alienation and lost child postures.

In blended families the children from previous marriages struggle for role position. Usually the first children have been filling in for the missing parent, when two single parents get together, the firsts are already out of one job. They then compete with each other for the first child role in the new system, even though they will remain the first child of the original parent. With infant death, miscarriage or still birth, the parents determine whether the child has a place. If parents talk about having five children and the third died at birth, then usually the next one is the fourth. Where there is a large period of time between births, the system still holds true. The second child is still the second child even though the first was born fourteen years earlier. The second child however might take on more responsibility issues and act in some first child capacities. A last child in a system also reacts differently because of being the last. They are more likely to be babied, indulged or fussed over. They may also feel victimized and helpless in a violent or neglectful system. They tend to deal with responsibility issues differently and can become self indulgent in later life. They may be the one expected to take care of others, especially aging parents.

EDUCATION

Educators may find it helpful to know the ordinal position of students and some generalities of learning styles. First kids tend to do better with clarity about the rules and expectations of the class. They are the ones who always read directions before tests. If the directions are clear they tend to do well. First kids do not really mind being taught in pieces such as dates or disconnected facts. They can feed them back. Seconds on the other hand need to know that in the discussion the feelings are being taken care of. The system feels good when the covert rules and expectations are not out of line, and they know feelings are going to be expressed appropriately and the feelings about the topic will also be taught or dealt with. Third kids essentially need to know they are liked and the relationship issues in the classroom are taken care of. If a teacher likes a third kid they do better in class. They also need a sense of the relationships between the parts of the class itself and each side of what ever is being taught is represented fairly. Thirds enjoy being the devil's advocate for the other side of things. Fourth kids do well if they know why they are there, and where they and the class are heading. If the teacher maintains a strong leadership role in the class and helps them see how this class fits in with goals, purposes of life, and career choices the fourth performs more to ability.

SYNOPSIS OF ORDINAL POSITION THEORY

Child Position One, Five, and Nine:
General Process:
- Responds to conscious explicit family rules.
- Follows dominant values and themes.
- Reacts to and identifies with father's system and values.
- Holds values and makes decisions in reaction to Father's system.

225

General Behavior:

- Other oriented, socially aware.
- Operates in explicit and obvious areas.
- Likely to act out of low self esteem.
- Action and responsibility oriented.

General Needs:

- Explicit and clear direction.
- Insight, rational or psychoanalytic therapies initially most effective.
- Support for noticing and accepting feelings and self worth.

General Goals:

- To increase capacity to integrate and synthesize.
- Establish realistic expectations of self.
- To detach some from external pressures and expectations.
- Lessen affective restriction and rule response.
- Develop own personal value system and nonperformance based self acceptance.

Child Position Two, Six and Ten:

General Process:

- Responds to covert unconscious rules.
- Reacts to and identifies with Mother's system and values.
- Responds to emotional process.

General Behavior:

- Acts out unconscious expectations and needs of others.
- Difficulty connecting affective and cognitive awareness resulting in puzzlement and seeming naive.

General Needs:

- To lessen swings between extremes.
- Focus on representational process such as fantasy, symbol and nonverbal growth technique such as role play, psychodrama, and media therapies (art, music, acting, movement).
- Naming and verbal descriptions are important, effective experiences are needed.
- Detachment from covert and unconscious feelings and needs of others.

General Goals:

- To heighten awareness of the covert and affective process.
- To develop congruency with affective and cognitive.
- Needs to develop a sense of control over responses, especially emotional.

Child Position Three, Seven, and Eleven:

General Process:

- Reacts to and identifies with marriage relationship.
- Internalizes familial relationship stress, especially the marriage.
- Difficulty with establishing a personal separate identity.

General Behavior:

- Primary concern is relatedness.
- May appear detached but is not.
- Feels ambivalent and has difficulty with choices.
- Will alter identity, values, and interests in different relationships.

General Needs:
- Identity formation.
- Emphasis on healthy relationship with some detachment internally while maintaining involvement externally.
- Responds to supportive relationship therapy, role playing.
- Needs support in decision making.

General Goals:
- Increased autonomy.
- More risk taking in relationship without losing separateness.
- Increased decisiveness.

Child Position Four, Eight, and Twelve:

General Process:
- Catches and collects unresolved family tension.
- Reacts to and identifies with family systems interaction.
- Attaches to whole system.

General Behaviors:
- Acts and feels responsible yet helpless and powerless.
- Acts and feels indulged, cute.
- May be disruptive.
- May follow questionable leadership.

General Needs:
- Sense of competency and focus in coping behaviors.
- Reality therapy, behavior modification.
- Strong direction, goals and leadership.

General Goals:
- Give up helplessness.
- Set personal goals and accept personal competency.
- Accept responsibility for self and relationship empowerment.

CHAPTER 19
STORIES

Telling the story is the song of love resonating
in open minds and hearts.

LEE'S STORY

As a young child, I was the mascot, the third born and the family fussed over me. I was the hope that some of the stress would be alleviated becoming the tension reliever. After a great run in that special place for six or seven years my younger brother was born taking over the role. I became a lost child. The family thought my brother was cuter, I did not think so. In baby pictures I definitely had the edge! I had a little boy version of the Shirley Temple look. Looking at my brother I saw a definite Winston Churchill look. However, it is difficult for a six year old to compete with a zero year old so I became a lost child and spent a few years without a place. I sat on the step with my friend saying, "What do you want to do?" and he replied, "I don't know, what do you want to do?" We said that for two years and did little. Eventually I discovered I could do well in school and sports, especially playing baseball, getting my name in the paper and consistently on the honor roll. I became the family hero, the star, an overachiever. This made my low functioning family look better but it did not make me feel much better. About that same time I discovered my mother needed a husband so I became my mother's surrogate spouse. I let her cry on my shoulder, I talked to her when she was in pain, I took care of her needs as best as I could. At nine years old I was married and had my first counseling client. I was doing marriage counseling and individual counseling. We could not get a group together although we might have tried! I call this emotional incest, my mother calls it career development. I also attempted to mediate the fights in the family so I became the family mediator. I learned my caretaker role and counseling role working with my mother and trying to talk my father out of drinking. I became a victim as well through the family violence that I could not effect any change over and continued to get hurt by. In sports I became an extension of my Dad. In some ways my athletic activities were less about me than about him. I think I was a reflection of the athlete he could have been or wanted to be but never pursued. I became an adolescent athletic burn out, a phenomena I have seen in many young people. At sixteen I dropped athletics for about ten years. I did not realize it at the time, but I could not enjoy athletics because the pressure was too much. I was not doing it for me, it was for my Dad. He did not attend my games, but I think it was something that made him feel good about him, but it did not help me feel good about me. I am very involved now with athletics but I know it is for me. My Dad is seventy and now he runs for himself, and I run for me. And sometimes we run together. The relationship has changed a great deal. I guess we have both grown.

Each role I played - mediator, mascot, extension of Dad, surrogate to Mom, victim, offender, enabler, over achiever, counselor, little parent to my younger brother, third kid all have had a residual impact on my life. When I am in pain or angry I would rather joke than fight or joke than cry. As a mascot, I tend to minimize my own feelings and sometimes the feelings of those around me. The clown learns to entertain or take care of other people's feelings. I still tend to perform more for others. As a lost child, I still wander around the country feeling disconnected and isolated. I travel too much. In fact I recently decorated my house to look like a Holiday Inn so I would feel at home when I am there! I bought a microwave so I could have airplane food at home. This is my continuation of the lost child role. I also tend to take care of other people more than myself. Of course my career choices speak for themselves, lay missionary, teacher, counselor. The residual impact of being in roles set up by someone else or by the family includes a difficulty knowing what I want, what my choices are. The impact of being the family hero, an overachiever, is I have had too much pressure in my life to achieve and frequently struggle with feeling good about what I do. It is my old role of trying to do good things to make the low functioning family have a sense of pride and community, to look good. As a hero I did not feel good about things done. Often after accomplishing something others may say was great I have a difficult time letting it in and feeling good. I had to accept that I cannot be my mother's counselor. I can care about her and make referrals but I do not try to do the counseling or fill in the missing gaps in her life.

In learning the victim role, I often felt buffeted about by the powers around me believing others were responsible for what was happening in my life. I often felt I could not impact my destiny and felt powerless. As a mediator I became involved in disputes I did not have a part of; mucking around in other people's business and relationship struggles. In the offending role, I have often inflicted other people with my own nasty moods, usually by withdrawing - the silence can be deafening. The collusion I have learned is an enabling posture where I have not always noticed the destruction around me or fight for the values I believe in.

As I learn about my past roles and see how they are replayed in my life I see more possibilities and choices open up. I still have many of the role tendencies but they no long have me.

The following is a brief chart of the roles played by the siblings in my family:

Older Sister	Older Brother	Me	Younger Brother
Little Princess	Scapegoat	Tension Reliever	Mascot
Victim	Hero	Lost child	Charmer
Abandoned One	Basement Child	Adventurer	Wild One
Lost Child	Rebel	Overachiever	Dad's Best Buddy
Quiet One	Robin Hood	Communicator	Confused
Good Child	Mom's Protector	Mediator	Crazy One
Little Parent	Collusive	Counselor	Sacrifice
Producer	Bad Seed	Victim	Strong One
Protector	Placater	Addict	Addict
Disciplinarian	Victim	Offender	Troubled
Religious Leader	Addict/Self	Extension of Dad	Rebel
Addict	Destructive	(Athlete)	Extension of Dad
Offender	Extension of Dad	Surrogate spouse	(Acting Out)
Dad's Protector	(Business)	(To Mom)	

My parents played roles as well in adulthood and childhood. Both were in addict and offender roles. They varied in terms of responsibility, care taking, and nurturing roles and were in combatant roles with each other. My Dad was the defiant one with a 'Raging Bull' role. My Mom played out martyrdom and sainthood. Their roles were learned in their original families just like mine. I still play a lot of these roles but at best I play them more than they play me.

RITA'S STORY

My mother was mentally ill. She had been diagnosed with schizophrenia and hospitalized but only for short periods. I was the reason she always got out. She was sick, but she was a loving mother, at least that is how the story went. I really needed for her to stay away. She would come out and be sweet and wonderful and quickly decide she didn't need medication. She would gradually begin to torture me; first with words and conflicting messages, then threats, then pinching and slapping, and eventually she would burn me, forcing my hand on a hot stove, or touching me with lit cigarettes. I never knew what was coming or whom she would be. My two older sisters had left me alone with her and I became the mother. I guess I became the husband too since she slept with me in my bed until I left home at twenty-three years old. Even with all of this I did well in school. I was competent in everything I attempted. I was a loner, fearing someone would find out about my mother if I got too close to them. I'm still competent and it is still difficult for me to open up. I've only recently considered dating. I've only been actively sexual a few times, and only with women. I don't know if I am Lesbian or not, I just can't image being close to a man. At least I couldn't until I began grieving the loss of my father. It was especially difficult because no one seems to know who he is. I thought it would be impossible to grieve what was never lost, because it never was. I also believe now I can have children and not hurt them, at least not intentionally, and I've stopped hurting myself, a job I took over from my mom after I left.

SUE'S STORY

My father was quite rigid and yet he was seen by everyone as gregarious and playful. My mother was labeled histrionic which I guess means she had feelings she didn't understand and couldn't deal with that would periodically overwhelm her. My father wasn't really gregarious, he was seductive; he wasn't really playful, he was lustful. My mother knew this emotionally which was part of her overwhelm and mine. I have hated my body and being a woman all of my life, I embarrass easily and have severe startle response, often feeling self conscious like I am being watched. I hate people looking at me.

A short time ago I was asked by a therapist a simple question: "How exactly did your father look at you?" I immediately numbed out, too frozen to answer, but in my mind a rapid fire series of images and awareness began cascading. We were not allowed to close doors, even our bedrooms and the bathroom doors always had to be open. We were told it was for safety. It wasn't. It was so my father could watch. My father was a voyeur. I now remember how I would often see his eyes on me while I was in the bathroom or preparing for bed. I learned to avoid those eyes and pretend he wasn't there, dissociating into another world. I have always been fascinated with incest, and now I must face it and do my healing. I often wished he had just gone ahead and touched me, maybe he did and I don't remember. But the hurt of being looked at in such an insidious way by my own father will take some time to heal. By the way, I too was becoming histrionic. I suspect my mother was hurt, not just by my father, but by someone in her childhood as well.

CARL'S STORY

I was raised on a farm, work was what we knew. I can say very little about my parent's except they worked hard. My father beat me severely but I didn't realize or remember that until recently. He died when I was eleven and I eulogized him in my memory, believing he would have protected me and nurtured me through adolescence had he lived. I lived with my fable for too long, I never grieved my loss nor dealt with the rage about the early abuse. I thought my anger was all about my uncle, my father's brother, who sexually molested me two days after my father's funeral. My mother completely fell apart after my dad's death. We, my brother and I, lived in thirteen different homes over the next seven years.

My uncle abused me for five of those years. He went to prison for other offenses, but came back last year. He moved close to where I now live with my second wife and her two daughters. I saw him shortly after he was released. I didn't speak but I reacted. I almost passed out and didn't know how I got home. That week I molested one of my daughters. I never even thought of such an act before. I turned myself in and still do not know what will happen to me. I now realize, though I am fully responsible for having hurt her, I was in a reexperiencing state as a result of my own trauma. I repeated what was done to me because I never completed what was done to me. I moved from the victim role to the offender role.

I did the same thing frequently with my anger. I would walk into a bar, drink and get into a fight usually hurting someone pretty badly. I needed to be angry at the people who hurt me but I didn't know it.

235

I was a rebel, defiant and at the same time a protector of my brother and my mother. I am a workaholic and over responsible. My life has changed so drastically now I only hope I can use my experience and new awareness to help someone else before more children get hurt and more adults stay hurt. I guess I'm still a protector making it very difficult to accept what I did. I turned myself in, although my daughter didn't want me to, and am awaiting sentencing. The powerlessness of this is currently overwhelming but I am using my time for healing. I have confronted the issue with my father and my uncle and am in the process of forgiving them because I know they were hurt just like I was.

JILL'S STORY

I was the first child in a very religious family. My father was a minister and my mother spent her adulthood being the 'minister's wife.' She volunteered for virtually every duty and need in the community. In community she was warm, gregarious and wonderful, in family she was cold and detached. I realize now she was angry at my father's emotional involvement with his flock and his emotional and sexual withdrawal from her.

I was a very plain child, at least I was led to believe so, and I dressed the part. My hair covered my face, my plain, bulky clothes covered my body. I believe I was an extension of my mother's physical and sexual shame that grew from her family and in the rejection of her marriage. Her rejection became my projection. As an extension of my mother I was led into service - without pay - for in our family system women have no real marketable talents or value.

She projected her coping strategy, her shame and her low self worth to me and I lived with her system as my shroud.

Because my parents were so busy taking care of the community I became the real parent to their other four children. I have never had children of my own, I thought it was a choice but now I realize and am saddened by the set up and burn out I experienced raising children who did not belong to me and being so blamed when they crashed. Our family looked perfect and now I know I could not show myself because I felt imperfect. My role as the quiet one was to not disturb my parents' perfect family image for inside I did not feel quiet. I have spent most of my life trying to make things that were not okay look okay. I have been the placater throughout my life. I have held a silent scream within me.

I also realize now I have held with my father's deep fear and spiritual crises and acted it out in my own religiosity. My father deeply questioned his belief and preachings and was afraid of being a fraud but would never expose his doubts to a healing light. I have lived a roller coaster of fear and doubt, on the crests being so religious as to drive people away, in the valleys stooped in despair and depression, a broken spirit.

I have made changes, my support system allows, hears and shares my doubts. I now am paid as a consultant for what I have done so long for free. I no longer hide my face, my body or my needs and I have began to let in the feedback I receive about my attractiveness. I will not have children and I grieve the loss but the child I am is awakening and I think I'll go out and play for awhile!

CHAPTER 20
Summary And Wintery

Roles are often unchosen ways one learns to adapt and survive dysfunction and abuse. All of the roles are dynamic and can change but also have a lasting impact. The role may have been left a long time ago but there is a residual effect and is fallen back on periodically or continues as a thread through life. Role overwhelm can occur causing a disintegration of personhood or lifestyle. Too many jobs, scattered commitments, secret lives, acting out, excess expectations all contribute to role overwhelm and result in burnout. The stress of this over time produces post stress reactions. Integrating and choosing a balanced lifestyle requires role noticing and careful role commitment. There is strength building in role function and formation.

Many roles involve a process similar to addiction, preventing feelings about the system or the role. To be able to change the roles, to be able to have choice the role must be made real, the feelings embraced. The role is a denial of true identity and emotional reality. Understanding role can facilitate choice for a style of life facilitating self discovery and identity. This involves taking risks by trying on new roles, keeping old ones that fit, and living with choices rather than sustaining the functioning of unhealthy systems. Genograms, reconstructions, sculpting or role playing the family to find out what effected us and what roles we and other members of the family played are common tools. This can be helpful but the family cannot easily be reconstructed. What is reconstructed or role played is a slice of time, a cross cut of the family. It does not reveal the *process* of the family.

Families are dynamic, organic and changing. Even in lower functioning families this change is constant. The roles at one point in the family, whether victim, caretaker, hero or clown may change entirely a few years later. One may feel betrayed or victimized by each parent at different times, begin taking care of Dad instead of Mom, or acting out, being rebellious and destructive after having been a hero. The roles and the family are changing and dynamic, the family is a process rather than a still life photo. We can portray an event and learn about the family system if we see each event as a *single* construct of family reality.

Childhood memories and stories will reflect the system. Themes of the family are perpetuated but the dynamics may change frequently. Roles are multiple. There are several categories of roles, changing and over lapping. Roles involve denial, lack of choice, feeling repression and a process of taking care of low functioning systems. They involve finding a place and survival within the system. Some are random, some consequential, some reactive, some chosen and some assigned. In the construct of the family, a slice of time can be valuable in giving insight, helping debrief, and experiencing feelings. It does not give the complete reality of life or the development of the system any more than watching one minute of a three act play gives the themes, plot, development and messages of the play. Actor's parts change as character develops. There are twists and turns in the play of personal living and family process.

A memory, a regression, a photo, an old letter, a visit with a knowledgeable person from the past gives input. These slices can stunt progress if treated as the *whole* of childhood. They can facilitate it by giving the data, the building blocks of the structure and awareness of the traumas of life that need debriefing. These offer glimpses of what drives, destroys and feeds compulsiveness and isolation. A complete video of childhood and family system isn't needed, but healing is a process of recovering as much reality as necessary to reclaim the lost childhood and lost child. A scene from childhood at age three does not tell the rules, hurts or losses experienced at six, nine or seventeen.

Memory is not the key to healing, but awareness and gentle acceptance is. Integrating the dynamics of development and the needs of individual unique process in recovery is crucial to the discovery of self. The primary roles of childhood must become real. Seeing the movement through these roles helps understand the patterns and dynamics of childhood. Finding the meaning, strength and gift of each role played can help in building healthy patterns.

The survival roles of childhood may be life debilitating but also create strengths discovered in the recovery of esteem and direction. The following are the positives to be learned from a low functioning system. Taken from *Finding Balance*, adults who have survived childhood in a low functioning family often develop these attributes:

- Ability to act well in chaos and can organize to avoid heavy fallout.
- Overachieving when needed to keep things from going to 'hell in a hand basket!'
- An ability to intuit the emotional state or needs of others that can keep things flowing smoothly.
- The ability to mediate differences can help the organization. Usually great at cleaning up messes.

- Skill at seeing through the false issues and the lies.
- Ability to see and understand shaming postures and unrealistic expectations.
- Refusal to accept abusive authority, an ability to 'sniff' it out and stand up to it.
- Ability to stand up and protect others, a refusal to accept injustice.
- Capable of intense loyalty.
- Can notice the needs of others.
- Become sensitive and can turn feelings into energy - anger and fear into strength and action.
- Will not shy away from a fight if there needs to be a fight.
- Will not run away from a tough project, even when it looks impossible.
- Responsibilities come naturally.
- After losing a 'big one,' one can get up again.
- Good at creative ways of getting things done.

Roles are not who we are, they are the parts we play. Find a good part and play it well.

INDEX

B

C

D

O

obsessive 130, 139, 196
Odd-Duck 175
offender 73, 98, 131, 136, 137, 147, 149, 151, 154, 155, 162, 167,
    168, 181, 182, 184, 186, 188, 189, 190, 191, 192, 193, 194,
    195, 196, 197, 198, 199, 200, 201, 202, 203, 230, 235
On Eagles Wings 205
Oracle 164
ORDINAL 205, 222, 225
Ordinal 207, 223
ordinal 224
Orphan 173
orphan 98, 161, 162, 171
Overachiever 155
overachiever 154, 156, 157, 208, 229, 231
Overt 45, 61, 144
overt 46, 61, 62, 63, 86, 99, 102, 126, 141, 149, 151, 155, 156,
    160, 172, 191, 208, 211, 213, 215

P

passive/aggressive 53, 159, 166
pathology 11, 23, 47, 50, 55, 100, 104, 109, 113, 115, 116, 125,
    126, 136, 147, 151, 152, 154, 156, 179, 219, 222
perpetrator 191, 193, 200, 202
Pirsig, Robert 80
Plain One 173
Pleaser 166
Poet 179
Politician 178
politician 131
Pollyanna 170
power 13, 31, 72, 75, 76, 98, 102, 107, 108, 109, 110, 111, 112,
    129, 137, 138, 147, 154, 160, 163, 166, 174, 178, 186, 188,
    189, 194, 195, 196, 198, 200, 202, 209, 210, 211, 218, 231

T

U

United States 5, 9

V

Victim 135
victim 51, 56, 57, 71, 73, 98, 102, 136, 137, 138, 143, 149, 154,
155, 175, 181, 182, 183, 184, 185, 186, 187, 188, 189, 190,
191, 192, 193, 194, 195, 196, 197, 198, 199, 201, 203, 230,
231, 235, 240
Viet Nam vii, 197
violence 11, 14, 18, 38, 59, 83, 87, 88, 107, 114, 115, 138, 142,
149, 155, 165, 179, 181, 182, 183, 186, 187, 188, 189, 197,
198, 199, 200, 201, 202, 203, 230
Voice Of Reason 177

W

Whitaker vii
Wisdom 107
wisdom 14, 48, 164
workaholic 146, 236

SELECTED REFERENCES

_____ (1964). "Prejudicial Scapegoating and Neutralizing Forces in the Family Group, With Special Reference to the Role of Family Healer." International Journal of Social Psychiatry (Congress):

_____ (1966). "Family Psychotherapy - Theory and Practice." American Journal of Psychotherapy **20**: 405-414.

_____ (1967). "The Individual and the Larger Contexts." Family Process **6**: 139-147.

Ackerman, N. (1966). Treating the Troubled Family. N.Y., Basic Books.

Alexander, P. C. and D. M. Schaeffer (1994). "A Typology of Incestuous Families Based on Cluster Analysis." Journal of Family Psychology **8**(4): 458-470.

Barker, R. G. (1968). Ecological Psychology: Concepts and Methods for Studying the Environment of Human Behavior. Stanford, Stanford University Press.

Berenson, D. (1976). Alcohol and the Family. Family Therapy: Theory and Practice Ed. P. Guerin. N.Y., Gardner Press. 284-297.

Bowen, M. (1978). Family Therapy in Clinical Practice. N.Y., Jason Aronson.

Bowen, M. (1978). The Use of Family Therapy in Clinical Practice. N.Y., Jason Aronson.

Brody, G. H. (1994). "Contributions of Family Relationships and Child Temperaments to Longitudinal Variations in Sibling Relationship Quality and Sibling Relationship Styles." Journal of Family Psychology **8**(3): 274-286.

Fincham, F. D. (1994). "Understanding the Association Between Marital Conflict and Child Adjustment: Overview." Journal of Family Psychology **8**(2): 123-127.

Graham-Bermann, S. A., S. E. Cutler, et al. (1994). "Perceived Conflict and Violence in Childhood Sibling Relationships and Later Emotional Adjustment." Journal of Family Psychology **8**(1): 85-97.

Green, R. J., Ph.D. and J. L. Framo Ph.D., Eds. (1981). Family Therapy: Major Contributions. Madison, CT, International Universities Press.

Grunwald, B. and H. McAbee. (1993). Guiding the Family: Practical Counseling Techniques. Muncie, IN. Accelerated Development, Inc.

Haley, J. (1963). Strategies of Psychotherapy. N.Y., Grune & Stratton.

Haley, J. (1970). "Approaches to Family Therapy." International Journal of Psychiatry **9**: 223-242.

Haley, J. (1973). Uncommon Therapy: The Psychiatric Techniques of Milton H. Erickson, M.D. N.Y., Norton.

Haley, J. (1975). Family Therapy. Comprehensive Textbook of Psychiatry Ed. H. I. K. Alfred M. Friedman & Benjamin J. Sadock. Baltimore, Williams & Wilkins.

Haley, J. (1976). Problem-Solving Psychotherapy. San Francisco, Jossey-Bass.

Harrison, M. E., Ph.D. (1994). Gender Identity Development. Amherst, University of Massachusetts Press.

Harrison, M. E. and T. L. Kellogg (1991). Hummingbird Words: Affirmations for Your Spirit to Soar and Notes to Nurture By. Santa Fe, BRAT,Inc.

Harrison, M. E. and T. L. Kellogg (1991). Roots and Wings: Notes on Growing a Family. Santa Fe, BRAT, Inc.

Harrison, M. E. and T. L. Kellogg (1992). Butterfly Kisses: Little Intimacies That Can't Be Bought, Sometimes Noticed, Sometimes Not. Santa Fe, NM, BRAT, Inc.

Harrison, M. E. and T. L. Kellogg (1994). Pathways to Intimacy: Communicating With Care & Resolving Differences. Santa Fe, BRAT, Inc.

Harrison, M. E. and T. L. Kellogg (1994). Reflections: Guideposts and Images for the Journey. Santa Fe, BRAT, Inc.

Hetherington, E. M. (1994). "Siblings, Family Relationships, and Child Development: Introduction." Journal of Family Psychology 8(3): 251-253.

Hoffman, L. (1981). Foundations of Family Therapy. N.Y., Basic Books.

Jackson, D. D. (1957). "The Question of Family Homeostasis." Psychiat. Quart. 31(Suppl.): 79-90.

Kellogg, T. L. (1990). Broken Toys Broken Dreams: Understanding & Healing Boundaries, Codependence, Compulsion, & Family Relationships. Santa Fe, BRAT, Inc.

Kellogg, T. L. and M. E. Harrison (1991). Finding Balance: 12 Priorities for Interdependence and Joyful Living. Deerfield Beach, FL, Health Communications, Inc.

Kellogg, T. L. and M. E. Harrison (1994). The Sacred Trust: Parenting and Guardianship of Children and Creating Healthy Families. Santa Fe, BRAT, Inc.

Keung Ho, M. (1987). Family Therapy with Ethnic Minorities. Newbury Park, Sage Publications.

Kramer, J. R. (1985). Family Interfaces: Transgenerational Patterns. N.Y., Brunner/Mazel.

Lussier, Y., S. Sabourin, et al. (1993). "On Causality, Responsibility, and Blame in Marriage: Validity of the Entailment Model." Journal of Family Psychology 7(3): 322-332.

McGoldrick, M. and R. Gerson (1986). Genograms in Family Assessment. N.Y., Norton Press.

Minuchin, S. (1974). Families and Family Therapy. Cambridge, Harvard University Press.

Minuchin, S. and A. Barcai (1969). Therapeutically Induced Family Crisis. Science and Psychoanalysis Ed. J. Masserman. N.Y., Grune & Stratton. 199-205.

Minuchin, S. and H. C. Fishman (1981). Family Therapy Techniques. Cambridge, Harvard University Press.

Minuchin, S., B. Montalvo, et al. (1967). Families of the Slums. N.Y., Basic Books.

Minuchin, S. et al. (1978). Psychosomatic Families. Cambridge, Harvard University Press.

Montalvo, B. and J. Haley (1973). "In Defense of Child Therapy." Family Process 12: 227-244.

Murphy, C. M. and T. J. O. (1994). "Factors Associated With Marital Aggression in Male Alcoholics." Journal of Family Psychology **8**(3): 321-335.

Pamela, C. A. and C. M. Schaeffer (1994). "A Typology of Incestuous Families Based on Cluster Analysis." Journal of Family Psychology **8**(4): 458-470.

Pearce, J. K. and L. Friedman, Eds. (1980). Family Therapy: Combining Psychodynamic and Family Systems Approaches. N.Y., Grune & Stratton.

Satir, V. (1965). "The Family as a Treatment Unit." Confina Psychiatrica **8**: 37-42.

Satir, V. (1972). Conjoint Family Therapy: A Guide to Theory and Technique. Palo Alto, Science & Behavior Books.

Satir, V. (1972). Peoplemaking. Palo Alto, Science & Behavior Books.

FROM THE AUTHORS

Life is a journey without a destination.
The journey itself is the destination.

Reflections

THE MULBERRY CENTER at The Welborn Hospital in Evansville, Indiana, and **ANACAPA HOSPITAL** in Port Hueneme, California are two of the places that are discovering a new, gentle means of giving people safety and support, to heal childhood trauma and build healthy identity while also dealing with their addictiveness. Through the efforts of several people in this field, treatment is changing and responding to the reality of our broken lives and broken dreams. I have found that I now make more referrals to treatment for the safety and gentleness of the setting than the confronting and breaking of denial of a disease. Many of us can benefit from something less than a three to six week residential experience. Outpatient groups, individual therapy, family counseling, couples counseling, often meeting once a week, can be an important part of this growth experience, but sometimes we need a safer setting, a more intense process. We need more support and community in an ongoing way. Nine years ago I began a program called the Compulsivity Clinics, which are now called Lifeworks Clinics, to deal with Adult Children issues, compulsive behaviors and codependency in an intense, safe, four and a half day process. This clinic involves information, small group experiential and personal process work. We keep the group size to six to eight people because I believe catharsis and emotional work should not be done with large audiences and groups. When we are doing this type of work, we should be the only one doing it, with other people around us for support. Kellogg's Lifeworks™ are held in different locations throughout the U.S. and Canada. Call 1-800-359-2728 for information.

In the **Kellogg's Lifeworks™** process I have learned about courage from the hundreds of individuals who face and embrace their demons, the courage of feeling and moving through hurts and trauma and the courage to change. There are many other short term programs available. I recommend checking around before deciding. Generally, they function as a renewal, a reinforcement and an integration. They are a great beginning for recovery and they can help us get unstuck at points along the way as we grow in our recovery. Other processes which facilitate our growth are conferences, books, tapes and meetings. The core of recovery lies within our sense of community with others in recovery. The strongest family of recovering people I know are in twelve step programs.

• **Life Balance™** is a two week clinic based on didactic and interactive process groups to assist people in finding resolution to disordered eating and body image problems. The Life Balance™ program is treatment designed and directed by Marvel Harrison, Ph.D. and Terry Kellogg, M.A., and THE MULBERRY CENTER Staff.

The Clinic is for those with one or more of the following:

• Lack of success with weight loss programs.
• A diagnosis of an eating disorder.
• A history of struggling with body acceptance.
• Emotional and overeating problems.
• A history of compulsive exercising.
• Restrictive eating habits.
• Health problems due to body weight.

The process integrates group therapy with focused action therapy, imagery, self reflection, journaling, physical activity, psych education and movement therapy in a safe environment. The personal sharing and connecting with others will help participants find a sense of balance and empowerment in their daily lives.

- **Life Connections**™ is an eight day process group specializing in Women's issues. Women struggling with life changes, depression, body image problems, or losses will find support and mobilizing tools for growth and renewal. Call 1-800-359-2728 for program dates, times, and details.

- **The Kellogg Harrison Intensive Treatment Program** at ANACAPA HOSPITAL is a safe and gentle therapy process designed to help each participant embrace their childhood, thereby deepening and broadening their recovery. This fourteen day program is based on didactic and interactive process groups to assist people in finding resolution. The intensive program integrates psychodrama, imagery, self reflection, journaling, physical activity, psycho-education and movement therapy in a safe environment of sharing and connecting with others to help participants find a sense of balance and empowerment in their lives.

This treatment is for those who are:

- struggling with issues of compulsive, addictive or self-defeating coping patterns.
- struggling with co-dependency and related intimacy issues.
- adult children of alcoholic or other dysfunctional families.
- survivors of emotional, physical, sexual, or spiritual abuse or neglect.

Call 1-800-359-2728 for program dates, times, and details.

- **The Resolution & Restoration™ Program:** Join us - **Terry Kellogg** and **Marvel Harrison** - in a place we call home, for a week of *Resolution* and *Restoration*. The setting is Harbour Island, a quaint and beautiful tropical place in the Bahamas with the world famous pink sand beach.

The Resolution & Restoration™ Program, an intensive therapy program will offer daily therapeutic process, information and experiential opportunities integrated with play and recreation adventures.

The therapy intensive will address issues for people struggling with:
- unresolved loss and grief
- emotional and overeating problems
- loss of interest and spirit
- trauma resolution
- intimacy and relationship issues
- compulsive/addictive or other self destructive behaviors
- self esteem problems
- disordered eating or poor body image
- anxiety or depression
- survivors of emotional, physical, sexual abuse and neglect

The process integrates group therapy with focused action therapy, imagery, self reflection, journaling, physical activity, and psycho-education in a safe environment. The personal sharing and connecting with others will help participants find a sense of balance and empowerment in their daily lives.

Interwoven with the therapy process will be daily meditation, beach walks and exciting opportunities and optional planned adventures including a deserted island picnic, beach activities, body surfing, snorkeling, scuba diving, fishing, dancing to Caribbean rhythms, sea kayaking, bicycling and more!

Call 1-800-359-2728 for program dates, times, and details.

Terry Kellogg and **Marvel Harrison** are also available to create a personalized therapy program for you or your group in your area or in New Mexico. Call 1-800-359-2728 to set up a program.

BRAT PUBLISHING ORDER BLANK

Mailing List & Order Blank—Please send books/tapes selected to:
(please print)

Name_____

Street_____

City_____ State/Province _____ Zip _____

Phone # Day _____ Evening _____
Make check/MO payable to BRAT Publishing or MC/VISA

#_____exp_____

Signature_____

# of Copies
BOOKS

_____ **Broken Toys Broken Dreams**: Terry Kellogg $10.95
_____ **Family Matters** *The Principles & Roles of Family* Terry Kellogg $11.95
_____ **Family Gatherings** *The Issues & Traits of Family* Terry Kellogg $11.95
_____ **AttrACTIVE WOMAN** *A Physical Fitness Approach To Emotional & Spiritual Well-Being*: Harrison & Stewart-Roache $8.95
_____ **Finding Balance:** *12 Priorities For Interdependence And Joyful Living* Kellogg & Harrison Family & Relationship Series $10.95
_____ **Pathways to Intimacy** *Communicating With Care & Resolving Differences* Kellogg Harrison Family & Relationship Series $7.95
_____ **The Sacred Trust** *The Parenting & Guardianship of Children and Creating Healthy Families* Kellogg Harrison Family & Relationship Series $7.95
_____ **Butterfly Kisses** *Little Intimacies For Sharing!* Harrison/Kellogg/Michaels $12.95
_____ **Hummingbird Words** *Self Affirmations Notes To Nurture By* Harrison/Kellogg/Michaels $12.95
_____ **Roots & Wings** *Words On Growing A Family* Harrison/Kellogg/Michaels $12.95
_____ **Reflections** *Guideposts and Images For The Journey* Harrison/Kellogg/Michaels $10.00

AUDIO/VIDEO TAPES

(Partial Listing—Please call for full brochure of
educational audios/videos on families and relationships)

_____ **Gentle Eating**-3 Audio Set: Marvel Harrison $24.00

_____ **Gentle Eating Experience**-Audio w/Manual Set: Marvel Harrison
$19.95

_____ **Creating Balance Audio**: Butterfly/Hummingbird/Roots Books on
tape with music $9.95

_____ **Trauma Tapes**-2 Audio Set: Terry Kellogg $15.95

_____ **Trauma Tapes**-2 Video Set: Terry Kellogg $59.90

_____ **Sexuality & Spirituality**-2 Video Set: Terry Kellogg $59.90

_____ **Family Roles** Video: Terry Kellogg $29.95

_____ **My Mother My Father Myself** Video: Terry Kellogg $29.95

_____ **Victimization Roles & Recovery** Video: Terry Kellogg $29.95

_____ **Broken Toys Broken Dreams** Video: Terry Kellogg $29.95

_____ **Codependency** Video: Terry Kellogg $29.95

_____ **Compulsive, Addictive Behaviors** Video: Terry Kellogg $29.95

_____ **Feelings: Learning to Live, & Love** Video: Terry Kellogg $29.95

_____ **Intimacy in Recovering Relationships** Video: Terry Kellogg $29.95

_____ **Shame and Recovery** Video: Terry Kellogg $29.95

Also Available from BRAT Publishing: marvel notes™ Elegant &
delightful greeting cards

Add $4.00 S/H per order please.

$_____ TOTAL ENCLOSED.

Mail or Fax to:
BRAT PUBLISHING, 369 Montezuma St., Suite 203, Santa Fe, NM 87501
505-662-9200 or 800-359-2728, Fax 505-662-4044

BRAT PUBLISHING ORDER BLANK

Mailing List & Order Blank—Please send books/tapes selected to:
(please print)

Name_____

Street_____

City_____ State/Province _____ Zip _____

Phone # Day _____ Evening _____
Make check/MO payable to BRAT Publishing or MC/VISA

#_____exp_____

Signature_____

# of Copies

BOOKS

_____ **Broken Toys Broken Dreams**: Terry Kellogg $10.95
_____ **Family Matters** *The Principles & Roles of Family* Terry Kellogg $11.95
_____ **Family Gatherings** *The Issues & Traits of Family* Terry Kellogg $11.95
_____ **AttrACTIVE WOMAN** *A Physical Fitness Approach To Emotional & Spiritual Well-Being*: Harrison & Stewart-Roache $8.95
_____ **Finding Balance:** *12 Priorities For Interdependence And Joyful Living* Kellogg & Harrison Family & Relationship Series $10.95
_____ **Pathways to Intimacy** *Communicating With Care & Resolving Differences* Kellogg Harrison Family & Relationship Series $7.95
_____ **The Sacred Trust** *The Parenting & Guardianship of Children and Creating Healthy Families* Kellogg Harrison Family & Relationship Series $7.95
_____ **Butterfly Kisses** *Little Intimacies For Sharing!* Harrison/Kellogg/Michaels $12.95
_____ **Hummingbird Words** *Self Affirmations Notes To Nurture By* Harrison/Kellogg/Michaels $12.95
_____ **Roots & Wings** *Words On Growing A Family* Harrison/Kellogg/Michaels $12.95
_____ **Reflections** *Guideposts and Images For The Journey* Harrison/Kellogg/Michaels $10.00

AUDIO/VIDEO TAPES

(Partial Listing—Please call for full brochure of
educational audios/videos on families and relationships)

_____ **Gentle Eating**-3 Audio Set: Marvel Harrison $24.00

_____ **Gentle Eating Experience**-Audio w/Manual Set: Marvel Harrison
$19.95

_____ **Creating Balance Audio**: Butterfly/Hummingbird/Roots Books on
tape with music $9.95

_____ **Trauma Tapes**-2 Audio Set: Terry Kellogg $15.95

_____ **Trauma Tapes**-2 Video Set: Terry Kellogg $59.90

_____ **Sexuality & Spirituality**-2 Video Set: Terry Kellogg $59.90

_____ **Family Roles** Video: Terry Kellogg $29.95

_____ **My Mother My Father Myself** Video: Terry Kellogg $29.95

_____ **Victimization Roles & Recovery** Video: Terry Kellogg $29.95

_____ **Broken Toys Broken Dreams** Video: Terry Kellogg $29.95

_____ **Codependency** Video: Terry Kellogg $29.95

_____ **Compulsive, Addictive Behaviors** Video: Terry Kellogg $29.95

_____ **Feelings: Learning to Live, & Love** Video: Terry Kellogg $29.95

_____ **Intimacy in Recovering Relationships** Video: Terry Kellogg $29.95

_____ **Shame and Recovery** Video: Terry Kellogg $29.95

Also Available from BRAT Publishing: marvel notes™ Elegant &
delightful greeting cards

Add $4.00 S/H per order please.

$_____ TOTAL ENCLOSED.

Mail or Fax to:
BRAT PUBLISHING, 369 Montezuma St., Suite 203, Santa Fe, NM 87501
505-662-9200 or 800-359-2728, Fax 505-662-4044